Lorna Doone

Dramatized for the Stage

Jill Hyem

A Samuel French Acting Edition

FOUNDED 1830

SAMUELFRENCH-LONDON.CO.UK
SAMUELFRENCH.COM

Copyright © 1997 by Jill Hyem
All Rights Reserved

LORNA DOONE is fully protected under the copyright laws of the British Commonwealth, including Canada, the United States of America, and all other countries of the Copyright Union. All rights, including professional and amateur stage productions, recitation, lecturing, public reading, motion picture, radio broadcasting, television and the rights of translation into foreign languages are strictly reserved.

ISBN 978-0-573-01827-5

www.samuelfrench-london.co.uk

www.samuelfrench.com

FOR AMATEUR PRODUCTION ENQUIRIES

UNITED KINGDOM AND WORLD
EXCLUDING NORTH AMERICA

plays@SamuelFrench-London.co.uk

020 7255 4302/01

Each title is subject to availability from Samuel French,
depending upon country of performance.

CAUTION: Professional and amateur producers are hereby warned that *LORNA DOONE* is subject to a licensing fee. Publication of this play does not imply availability for performance. Both amateurs and professionals considering a production are strongly advised to apply to the appropriate agent before starting rehearsals, advertising, or booking a theatre. A licensing fee must be paid whether the title is presented for charity or gain and whether or not admission is charged.

The professional rights in this play are controlled by The Agency Ltd, 24 Pottery Lane, Holland Park, London W11 4lZ.

No one shall make any changes in this title for the purpose of production. No part of this book may be reproduced, stored in a retrieval system, or transmitted in any form, by any means, now known or yet to be invented, including mechanical, electronic, photocopying, recording, videotaping, or otherwise, without the prior written permission of the publisher. No one shall upload this title, or part of this title, to any social media websites.

The right of Jill Hyem to be identified as author of this work has been asserted by her in accordance with Section 77 of the Copyright, Designs and Patents Act 1988

CHARACTERS

Ridds:
John (senior)
John (junior)
John, aged 12
Sarah, John's mother
Annie, John's sister
Annie, aged 10
Lizzie, John's sister
Lizzie, aged 8
Tom, a cousin
Betty, a servant
Jem, a farm labourer
First Farmer
Second Farmer
Third Farmer

Doones:
Lorna
Lorna, aged 9
Ensor
Counsellor
Carver, Counsellor's son
Charlie
Will
Hal
Gwenny, Lorna's maid
Ensie, as young a child as possible
Woman at fire

Others:
Jeremy, the King's envoy
Judge
Spank, his clerk
Benita, an innkeeper's wife
Kirke
Parson
Margery Badcock
Man on battlefield

Farmers, labourers, Doones, soldiers, wedding guests

SYNOPSIS OF SCENES

ACT I

Scene 1	Exmoor. 1673
Scene 2	Plovers' Barrows' Farm. Two days later
Scene 3	Sir Ensor's House. Doone Valley
Scene 4	Plovers' Barrows' Farm. Spring 1674
Scene 5	Exmoor. Waterfall. Next day
Scene 6	Meadow. Doone Valley
Scene 7	Plovers' Barrows' Farm. Summer 1674
Scene 8	Meadow. Lorna's Bower. February 1683
Scene 9	Plovers' Barrows' Farm. Three weeks later
Scene 10	London. Judge Jeffreys' Chamber. Summer 1683
Scene 11	Meadow. Lorna's Bower. Two weeks later
Scene 12	Sir Ensor's House. Night
Scene 13	Seven Rooks' Nests. Winter 1683
Scene 14	Sir Ensor's House

ACT II

Scene 1	Plovers' Barrows' Farm. January 1684
Scene 2	Sir Ensor's House. Next day
Scene 3	Plovers' Barrows' Farm
Scene 4	Plovers' Barrows' Farm. Spring 1684
Scene 5	Exmoor
Scene 6	Plovers' Barrows' Farm. Next day
Scene 7	Battlefield. June 1685
Scene 8	An Inn
Scene 9	Plovers' Barrows' Farm. A few months later
Scene 10	Doone Valley
Scene 11	Oare Church. Spring 1686
Scene 12	Exmoor
Scene 13	Plovers' Barrows' Farm

Suggested doubling of rôles

Some cast doubles may be used if desired. I suggest the following:

John Ridd (senior) / Judge Jeffreys
Jem Fry / Colonel Kirke
First Farmer / Parson Bowden
Second Farmer / Spank
Third Farmer / Man on battlefield
Gwenny / Margery Badcock
Betty Muxworthy / Woman at fire

Jill Hyem

GENERAL NOTES

The tale of *Lorna Doone* with its irresistible blend of adventure and romance has become a lasting legend.

This fairy tale quality is, I believe, essential to the success of a stage production since it cannot compete with the more naturalistic versions of film and television.

The stage effects and main production sequences (snow storm, battles, waterfall, etc.) should have a magical quality and a deliberate theatricality. Thus, as if by magic, a table may become a cart or a barrel a horse.

There should be a large dressing-up basket at the side of the stage from which characters can take jackets, cloaks, bonnets, soldiers' uniforms, etc. whenever a change of costume is necessary.

However it is staged, it is essential that the story of John Ridd's love for Lorna Doone should remain firmly at the heart of the play. They are a hero and a heroine in the same mould as Romeo and Juliet. The audience should be able to weep unashamedly when Lorna is shot at the end, and if anyone wants to hiss at Carver Doone and his comrades, so much the better.

The Great Outdoors, also essential to the story, must be conjured up, not only by the ingenuity of set, props and lighting, but also by the use of pastoral sounds and music throughout.

John Ridd should not be a static Narrator but will walk in and out of the action as he relives his story.

Jill Hyem

BACKGROUND HISTORY

1660   Charles II was restored to the throne. While in exile in the Netherlands he sired an illegitimate son.

Soon after Charles's return his handsome son, the Duke of Monmouth, came to England. He became very popular, and as he grew up people began to call him "the Protestant Duke" to distinguish him from the King's brother, the Duke of York, who was a Roman Catholic. As Charles had no legitimate heirs, York was heir to the throne. However, he was very unpopular as few people wanted a Roman Catholic king.

1683   During this year there were plots against the throne and Monmouth thought it best to flee to the Netherlands in case he should be accused of taking part.

1685   In February Charles II died and the Duke of York succeeded him as James II. On 11th June Monmouth landed at Lyme Regis (Dorset), with a few followers and claimed that he was the rightful king. By the time he reached Taunton (Somerset) he had an army of some thousands of men and had himself proclaimed king. However, his men were mostly peasants armed only with scythes and they had to fight against James's trained soldiers.

The rebels made a night attack on James's army camped at Sedgemoor (Somerset) but were driven off and slaughtered. Monmouth was later captured and beheaded on Tower Hill on 15th July. Other rebels were tried before Judge Jeffreys, the Lord Chief Justice, on his notorious Bloody Assize.

ACT I

Scene 1

Exmoor. A moonlit night. 1673

A mist hangs over the moor. A rocky ridge rises up in the distance. The skeleton of a tree in the foreground. To begin with we hear only the sound of a tumbling stream nearby and the bleating of sheep in the distance

Then John Ridd appears through the mist. NB: Since he is playing himself in the play as well as narrating the story, we must assume that he is telling it no more than ten years after the end of the play. Any age difference should therefore be indicated only in a maturity of manner

John (*as Narrator, with a slight West Country accent*) It was on just such a night as this that the Doones first came into my life and changed it forever. I had heard of them before, of course. Everyone in these parts had heard of the Doones of Bagworthy Vale (*pronounced Badgery*), thieves and outlaws as they were. (*With emotion*) And murderers too, as my family were soon to... But I am leaping ahead. In spite of their rough and murdering ways, the Doones were of noble birth. You may wonder how they came to be outlawed. Back in sixteen forty when the troubles were starting in England, Sir Ensor Doone fell out with his cousin, Lord Lorne, over some jointly inherited land. They took the case to law, hoping to have the estate fairly apportioned, but instead of dividing the land, they were soon divided *from* it. (*Beat*) Lord Lorne was still quite well-to-do, but Sir Ensor was left near penniless. He determined to see the King—Charles the First—hoping he would find fair hearing at court. But he found only further disgrace. (*Beat*) For in his bitterness Sir Ensor insulted everyone. Saying things beyond forgiveness. Some say he swore at King Charles himself, and that was why he was outlawed. Others say it was because he slew a gentleman at court who had a hand in his hardship. Accounts vary! But one thing is sure, Sir Ensor was made a felon outlaw. (*Beat*) He resolved to settle in some outlandish place where none would know him. And so he came to Exmoor, alas the day. Yet had he not, I should never have met my sweet love and... But not so fast! At first there were only a few of Sir Ensor's band, and the country folk brought offerings to them. A side of bacon. A keg of cider. A brisket of venison. But when the newness of his coming began to wear off, folk were apt to think that even a gentleman should work, or pay others for doing so. (*Beat*) As the young Doones grew up—tall and fierce as Goliaths—they began to take things without asking. Not just sheep and cattle either. They carried off many a farmer's daughter to add to their stock. (*Beat*) But that was not the worst they did ... as you will soon learn...

John disappears as the mist swirls him up

Pause. Then we discern the sound of men's voices singing some way off. The song is a stirring hymn, the singers a small group of farmers returning from market. The singing becomes louder as the farmers approach from the back of the auditorium

> *They enter (on horseback), carrying goods they have bought at the market. They are led by John Ridd (senior). He is a large good-looking man in his late thirties. He carries a staff, as the others do. They will all speak with West Country accents. Suddenly the singing starts to peter out and the farmers halt in their tracks*

First Farmer Look! Up there on the ridge.
Second Farmer Oh my God.

We see, with them, the shadows of some horsemen outlined against the sky

Ridd The Doones.
Third Farmer Merciful Father.
First Farmer Quick. Let us turn back before they see us.
Second Farmer And put a bullet through us like as not.

> *As they start to turn back a man steps out of the mist holding a gun. He is Charlewood Doone (Charlie), tall, well-built, in his early twenties*

Charlie (*with the voice of breeding common to all the Doones*) Good evening to you, gentlemen.
First Farmer (*doffing his hat subserviently*) Good evening, sir.

The others, except John Ridd, doff their hats too and mumble greetings

Charlie And where might you be going at this hour?
Second Farmer Home, sir.
Third Farmer To Oare, sir.
Charlie I think not. Not, that is, until you have handed over your purses.
First Farmer Please, sir, we are but poor farmers who——

Act I, Scene 1   3

Charlie Poor be damned. I'll wager your purses are stuffed full after a day at Porlock Market. Throw them on the ground, and you will come to no harm.
Second Farmer (*aside*) Best do as he bids.

They go to take out their purses, but are stopped by John Ridd

Ridd No, wait, my friends! Why should we give our hard-earned money to these villains?
Charlie (*swaggering over to him*) And who might you be, Clod, that dares challenge a Doone?
Ridd I am John Ridd. A peaceful man and an honest one, which is more than can be said of you.
Charlie (*brandishing his gun*) Hold your tongue or I will silence you for good.
First Farmer (*aside*) Do as he says, John.
Charlie (*to the others*) Your purses now before I take them from you.
Ridd (*stopping them again*) No! (*To Charlie*) If you were without, we would give you money, for we are God-fearing men. But you have clothes on your back and food in your bellies, why should you take from us? We have wives and children to feed and——
Charlie Children who will soon be fatherless if you don't do as I bid. Your purses! Under that tree there. And be fast about it.
First Farmer Yes, sir.
Second Farmer At once, sir.

The farmers, except John Ridd, hurry over to the tree and lay down their purses, then hurry off

Only the Third Farmer lingers at a distance, waiting for Ridd

Charlie (*to Ridd*) Your purse, Clod. I am waiting.
Third Farmer Go on, John. Give it to him.

Ridd holds his ground

Charlie (*brandishing the gun*) I said your purse.
Ridd If you want it, come and take it. And in a fair fight too. Unless you are a coward as well as a thief. (*To the farmer*) Seth, give him your staff.

Charlie hesitates, then throws the gun down and grabs the staff from the trembling farmer. He and Ridd face each other

Charlie All right, Master Ridd. Let's see your mettle.

They fight. It is soon apparent that Ridd is skilled at single-stick, and before long he knocks Charlie to the ground

He is about to pick up the gun when two other Doones (Will and Hal) appear out of the mist, tall and threatening

Third Farmer Look out, John.

Ridd turns and sees them

The Third Farmer scuttles off

Ridd takes on both men, and after a fierce fight eventually knocks them both unconscious. He dusts himself down. Charlie starts to come to

Ridd Let that be a lesson to you. And to the rest of your kin. (*He picks up Charlie's gun, gathers up the purses and turns towards home*)

A shot rings out. John Ridd, hit in the back, staggers, then turns towards the ridge. The moon spotlights a solitary horseman outlined against the sky, his gun aloft. John Ridd falls to the ground, dead

SCENE 2

Plovers' Barrows' Farm. Two days later

The set comprises the farm kitchen and the yard leading to it. The kitchen is a large room. It is the centre of the house. There is a table and chairs, a large oven, a fire burning in the grate. Long sides of bacon are hanging up to smoke. We hear sheep bleating off. A dog barking. Hens

In one of the chairs sits Sarah Ridd. She is a pretty, plump woman in her thirties, currently in mourning. So too is Betty Muxworthy, an elderly servant who is busy at the oven. Beside Sarah sits Lizzie, aged eight. She is small and skinny. The brains of the family, she will be taking in everything during the following

Jem Fry, a farm worker of about fifty, enters the yard with John Ridd (junior), aged twelve

John *Now* will you tell me, Jem? Now we have stabled the horses.
Jem (*evasively*) Tell 'ee what, lad?

Act I, Scene 2

John You know what! Why you have fetched me home from school when the holidays don't start for another two weeks? And why Father did not come as he usually does?

Jem walks on

(*Persistently*) And if he could not come, why didn't he meet us at the telling house or the crooked post? Has he gone to Taunton on business? Or have we guests? Is that it?
Jem You ask too many questions, John.
John Then answer them!
Jem They're not for me to answer.

Annie comes out of the farmhouse. She is John's eldest sister, aged ten, pretty and sweet-natured. The two are very close

John There's Annie. She will tell me. (*He runs to her*) Annie! What's the secret? Why have they fetched me home from school?

She starts to weep

Sister, what is it? Don't cry. Look I have brought you some sweetmeats.

Annie turns and runs into the farmhouse. John and Jem follow her

Annie Oh Mother, he's back.
John (*close on her heels*) Annie, what's up? Hello, Mother. Betty. Did you see the fine greeting she... (*He breaks off as he sees their faces*) What's happened? Where's Father? (*He notices their clothes*) Why are you dressed like that?

Sarah smothers a sob

(*As it sinks in*) No...
Sarah Yes, son. He's dead. Your father's dead.
Betty Murdered by the Doones of Bagworthy, rest his soul.
John Murdered?
Jem On his way home from market on Saturday. That was what I could not tell 'ee, lad.
John (*still unable to take it in*) But I bought him a new pipe in Tiverton yesterday. (*He takes it out of his pocket*)
Sarah He'll have no use for that now, son. (*She starts to weep*) Oh, John, John, why *you*? There was never a better husband.

John goes to comfort her

Betty Nor a better master. I nursed him as a lad and made his clothes, and now I must dress him for his coffin.
Jem Hush, Betty Muxworthy, don't *you* start.
Betty Don't you hush me, Jem Fry, great oaf that you are!

John hurls the pipe into the fire, then turns back to others with emotion

John Who killed him? Which of the Doones was it?
Jem We know not. Only that he was shot down.
Betty It matters not which, they are all villains.
Sarah Oh yes, it does. They have a right to know who murdered their father, and to see justice done.
Jem There be no justice where the Doones are concerned.
Betty Ay, no one dare meddle with them.
Jem They're too strong by number.
Betty And too high by birth.
Sarah They do say Sir Ensor is a gracious gentleman. (*She summons up courage*) I shall go to the Doone Gate and demand to see him.
Jem Go to Bagworthy Forest?
Betty To see Sir Ensor Doone?
Annie No, Mother!
Betty Poor soul, her grief has turned her mind.
Sarah No, Betty, I am in my full senses. I shall go there now this very day. Annie, fetch my cloak.
Annie But Mother——
Sarah Do as I say.
Jem Nay, Mistress, I beg you. Set foot there and they'll like as not murder you too.
Annie Oh no, please!
Sarah It's all right, Annie. Even a Doone would not harm a woman in widow's garb. *You* fetch my cloak, Lizzie.

Lizzie goes and returns with a black cloak

Betty Wait, Mistress, for the love of God. Suppose Sir Ensor does agree to see you—which I doubt—what will you say to him? You a common farmer's wife and he a titled gentleman?
Jem Ay. How can you charge a kinsman of his with such a foul deed?
Sarah You think I should overlook the matter of John's death because his murderer has a title? (*She puts on the cloak*) John, look after your sisters while I am gone.

Act I, Scene 3

John No, Mother. Betty and Jem will attend them. I am coming with you.

They all look at him

(*With new authority*) Father would have wished it.

John and Sarah go off

Doones bring on Sir Ensor's throne chair and other props

Scene 3

Sir Ensor's House. Doone Valley. Later the same day

The set comprises Sir Ensor's day room and the approach to the houses in Doone Valley. Sir Ensor's house is bigger than the rest. A plank bridge leads to it across a stream. The room is bare. Only the throne chair and a few other signs of his former station. Perhaps a piece of tapestry and some leather books

After a moment, Will Doone approaches the house from a steep path that leads down to the valley

Will (*calling back to someone at the top of the path*) Wait there till I bid you come. (*He crosses the bridge and raps on Sir Ensor's door*)

After a moment, Sir Ensor appears. He is a tall, aristocratic old man with long white hair. In spite of the billhook he holds in his hand and the hedger's gloves he wears, he is every inch a gentleman

Ensor (*peering*) Which of you is it?
Will Will, sir. There is a woman asking to see you.
Ensor (*sighing*) Not another!
Will She came to the entrance gate with a young boy.
Ensor What have you lads been up to this time?
Will Nothing, sir.
Ensor Would that I live to see *that* day. Where is she?
Will Waiting up by the rowan tree.
Ensor What? You brought her here? Into our valley?
Will Have no fear, sir. We covered their eyes.
Ensor Bring her down then. (*He turns back into the room*) I know young men will be young men, but I am tired of sorting out these escapades. (*He goes inside*)

Will whistles to Hal, who appears at the top of the path leading John and Sarah, who are both blindfolded

Hal Careful, there is a steep path down.
Will You can uncover their eyes now, Hal.

Hal removes the blindfolds. Sarah and John look with amazement at the valley

Hal Like our houses, do you?
Will Make haste. Sir Ensor is waiting.

They lead Sarah and John to the bridge

Across there.

Sarah and John cross the bridge. The two Doones will play dice together during the following

Sarah (*hesitating nervously at the door*) Perhaps we should not have come.
John (*steeling himself*) I will knock. (*He knocks and steps back quickly as—*)

Sir Ensor comes to the door

Ensor Good day to you, madam.
Sarah G-g-good day, sir. (*She bobs*)
Ensor (*impatiently*) Well, good woman? What has brought you hither?
Sarah Well sir, it's—I am loath to—you see——
John We are here to ask about my father. Sir.
Ensor (*with dry humour*) You have left the matter rather late, have you not? This lad must be nigh on twelve years.
Sarah I know not what you mean. (*She starts to weep*) My husband is gone, that is all I understand. And it was *your* men who did it.

John puts his arm round her

Ensor Madam, I crave your pardon. My eyes are old or I should have known. (*To John*) Bring your mother inside, boy.

They follow Sir Ensor into the house

(*Indicating the chair*) Pray be seated.
Sarah No, sir. I could not sit down in the house of those who robbed me of my husband.

Act I, Scene 3

Ensor Do not distress yourself, madam. If we have your husband prisoner, he shall go free without ransom because I have insulted you.

Sarah lets out a wail

You are a hard woman to please.
John You do not understand, sir. My father is not a prisoner. He is dead. Murdered.

Ensor turns to look at him

By one of your kinfolk.
Sarah (*restraining him*) Hush, John! Loath would I be, Sir Ensor, to accuse anyone unfairly. But I have lost the very best husband God ever gave to woman.
Ensor Madam, I——
Sarah (*carried away*) I knew him when he was but the age of John here. He taught me all I know. When it was best to kill a pig and how to treat maidens.
Ensor Indeed he sounds——
Sarah (*continuing over*) All the herbs he left to me and all the bacon curing. And never an unkind word he spoke——
Ensor He must have been a——
Sarah Nor stopped me short of speaking! (*She weeps again*) Oh John, John! Saturday morning I was a wife, and Saturday night a widow and my children fatherless.
Ensor What was your father's name, boy?
John John Ridd, sir. And there was not a finer or better man in Somerset or Devon.
Ensor (*looking closer at John*) And where did this ... mishap befall?
John He was coming home from Porlock Market, sir.
Sarah With a new gown for me and a shell to put my hair up. Oh John, how good you were to me!
Ensor Madam, this matter shall be attended to at once. My boys are a little wild, I know, yet I cannot think they would willingly harm anyone.
Sarah They harmed my John. Did I not wash his bleeding body?
Ensor (*going to the door*) If any wrong has been done, I will redress it to my utmost. (*He calls*) Will!
Will Yes, sir?
Ensor Send Counsellor to me.
Will At once, sir. (*He moves off and calls*) Send Counsellor to Captain!

Someone off repeats "Send Counsellor to Captain". We hear the instruction echoing round the valley

Ensor (*turning back to Sarah*) Counsellor is our record and our judge. He is cognizant of all that happens here and is very stern against us if a wrong is committed. Will you not be seated now? I am sure your good husband would not wish you to suffer further discomfort.

A pause

Sarah Thank you, sir. (*She sits*)

John stands protectively beside her

Ensor (*to John*) You are a sturdy lad, as well as an outspoken one.
Sarah It was his grief speaking, sir. He is a good hard-working boy. *And* he can read and write.
Ensor Indeed.
Sarah In Latin.
Ensor Is that so?
Sarah And Greek too.
John (*modestly*) Only six words of Greek, Mother.
Sarah My husband is a great admirer of learning. *Was* I should say. Oh dear, I still can't grasp it! John here, being his only son, he sent him to be schooled in Tiverton! (*Proudly*) At Master Peter Blundell's school.
Ensor I have heard of it.
Sarah But now all that will have to end. He will be needed on the farm. I have only two daughters else, and they be younger than he.
Ensor This is a sorry business.

Counsellor Doone appears. He is an enormous, square man, his girth making up for his lack—by Doone standards—of height. He has a very long grey beard

Counsellor (*to Will*) Is Captain in his cottage?
Will Yes, Counsellor.

Counsellor begins to cross the bridge

Ensor Ah, is that Counsellor I hear?
Counsellor Good day, Captain. How may I serve you?
Ensor Come in, Counsellor. I need your advice. Here is a lady of good repute.
Sarah Oh no, sir, not a lady. Only a woman.
Ensor Allow me, madam, by our leave. Here is a lady, Counsellor, of great repute in this part of the country, who charges the Doones with unjustly slaying her husband.

Act I, Scene 3

Counsellor Does she indeed?
Sarah Yes, sir. And it was murder too, if ever there was murder.
Counsellor The perfect right and truth of the case is all I wish to know, madam. Then justice shall be done.
Sarah Oh sir, I pray you, make no great bones of it. Only look at me and my poor son and you will know the truth.
Counsellor Justice, madam, is based on hard facts, not soft countenances. (*Sternly*) Put the case.
Sarah (*nervously*) Well, sir — it happened this way — that is — it is not easy to — —
Ensor The case is this, Counsellor. This lady's husband was slain, she claims, upon his return from Porlock Market last Saturday night. Amend me if I am wrong, madam.
Sarah Sometimes it seems a twelvemonth, sometimes an hour.
Counsellor But it *was*, nonetheless, last Saturday night?
Sarah Yes, sir.
Counsellor Cite your husband's name.
Sarah John Ridd, sir.
Ensor We have heard of him, Counsellor. A worthy man who meddled not with our duties.
Sarah He was a churchwarden too, sir. And a sober man. He would have no company with any who went beyond half a gallon of beer.
Counsellor *If* we might continue.
Ensor Now Counsellor, if any of our boys have been rough, they shall answer it dearly. Tell us the truth of the matter if you know it.
Sarah Oh Sir Counsellor, only tell me who it was shot my poor husband down, and I will bless you, sir.
Counsellor (*stopping her*) Please, madam. (*To Sir Ensor*) I will be brief, Sir Ensor. For I am well versed of this matter. The facts are these. Three or four of our best behaved gentlemen went to Porlock Market on Saturday with a lump of money. They bought some household stores and comforts there. At a very high price too! Later they pricked upon the homeward path. Avoiding vulgar revellers. As they drew bridle to rest their horses, a robber set upon them. A man of great size and strength. Since their goods were on trust to them, they would not give them up without a blow. But the power of this rogue was terrible. He had soon smitten three of our men senseless. Whereupon the last of them tried to ward off his blows with a pistol. Carver it was, sir. Our brave and noble Carver. Who saved the lives of his brethren. But not with the intention to kill. Dear me, no. In spite of the fellow's savage attack on his comrades, Carver prayed it might be only a flesh wound.
Sarah (*shaken*) No ... no ...
John (*equally aghast*) It cannot be ...

Ensor I am afraid it is. If Counsellor reports it so. (*Businesslike*) We are always glad to explain any misapprehension that you rustic people may be under.
Sarah Not John ... he *would* not.
Ensor We will not add to your grief and shame, madam, by charging your poor husband with any set purpose of robbery.
Counsellor What about his land, Captain? Will we be bringing a suit for attainder of his property?
Sarah Oh no, sir, please! The farm is all we have.
Ensor No, Counsellor, we will forbear. Even an honest man may use his staff mistakenly in this uncharactered age of rape and violence.
Sarah (*almost unable to speak*) Come, John. We have no further business here. (*She goes to the door*)

John follows, then turns back to Counsellor

John My father was no robber.
Counsellor Begone, boy, before Sir Ensor decides to be less merciful.

Sarah and John go. They cross the bridge during the following

Will that be all, Captain?
Ensor That will be all, Counsellor.

Counsellor goes. Sir Ensor looks after him, then turns to get a small leather bag out of a drawer

Counsellor (*calling to Will and Hal as he crosses the bridge*) Take them back to the entrance gate, and make sure they return no more.
Will Yes, Counsellor.

Counsellor departs by the way he came

(*To Hal*) Cover their eyes.
Ensor (*calling from the door*) Will? Come here.

Will goes to him. They exchange a few words that we do not hear and Sir Ensor hands him the leather bag

Hal (*to Sarah*) Come, madam, let me blindfold you again.
Sarah My eyes are blind enough with weeping.
Will Wait, Hal, I have something for her.

Sir Ensor goes back into the house. Will crosses the bridge and holds out the leather bag for Sarah

Captain sends this for you, madam. He says it is for the little ones.

Sarah looks at it and takes it. We hear the sound of coins. Then she flings it on to the ground as if it were contaminated

Sarah It was not money I came for. It was the truth. (*To Hal*) Cover my eyes and lead us from this evil place.

Hal covers her eyes, while Will does the same to John. Then they lead them up the path from whence they came

A pause

Carver Doone steps out of the shadows. He is a massive man, dark, bearded, formidable. He stands watching after John and Sarah, a malicious smile on his face. Then he strides over to where the leather bag lies discarded on the ground. He picks it up, pockets it and strides away

Scene 4

Plovers' Barrows' Farm. Six months later. Spring 1674

Betty Muxworthy and Annie are busy preparing dinner. Lizzie sits by the hearth, her head in a book

We hear gunshots off in the distance

Betty I hope he be doin' no damage up there.
Annie He's only shooting at the old ash tree, Betty.
Betty Last time he did that he brought down the church gutter.
Annie He is more practised now.
Betty With Jem Fry for teacher, he had best practise *ducking*. Now Lizzie, will you take your head out of that book and stir your mother's broth.
Lizzie Oh, may I not finish the page?
Betty Your poor mother lies ailing, and you think only of books.
Lizzie Just two more sentences.
Betty Why can't you be like Annie here? She has a turn for cooking and no mistake.

Annie Lizzie has a turn for reading.
Betty What good ever came of reading? She won't find a husband by reading. Not that I believe in it.
Lizzie Reading or husbands?
Betty Reading, Mistress Goose. How could anyone make sense of all those squiggles and dots? See that page? It looks like a pig with measles. Folk who say they can read are nothing more than liars.
Lizzie Even Parson Bowden?
Betty The Parson be only a man same as the rest of 'em, and all men are pretenders.

John comes through the yard, carrying his gun

(*To Lizzie*) Come, take the ladle.

Lizzie does so reluctantly. John comes into the kitchen holding the gun so that it points at Betty

John Is dinner ready?
Betty (*putting up the frying pan for protection*) Stop! Put that thing down before you shoot me dead.
John It's all right, Betty. D'you think I don't know how to handle a gun? The muzzle is on—look. It would never shoot you unless I pulled the trigger with the crook of my little finger——
Betty Stop, Jack, stop!
John Don't worry, the only person I will ever shoot is one by the name of Carver Doone.
Betty You'd do better listening to your mother, and let God take revenge on him.
John How *is* Mother?
Betty Not much recovered, poor soul.
John Will she still not eat?
Betty Only a little broth. Keep stirring, Lizzie.
Annie I wish there was something we could tempt her with.
Betty Ay. 'Tis not good to have no love of your victuals.
John There must be some delicacy we could fetch for her.
Annie I cannot think of anything.
Lizzie How about some loaches?

They look at her

Remember that time you brought some back in a jar from Tiverton, John?
John Oh yes, I caught them myself in the Lowman river.

Act I, Scene 5

Annie And you baked them, Betty, with vinegar and bay leaves and peppercorns.
Betty I mind it well. Your mother said she had never tasted anything to compare with them.
John Well done, Lizzie! You have hit on the very thing. Tomorrow I shall go fishing. (*He picks up his fishing gear*)

He and Annie move to the stream

Scene 5

Exmoor. Waterfall. Next day

The Light should indicate a cold spring day. We hear the sound of water. Sheep bleating. Birdsong

John is standing in a stream, bare-legged, his sleeves rolled up. He has a rod with a three-pronged fork attached to the end of it. Annie sits on a rock, watching. Beside her are John's shoes and socks and a basket for the fish

John (*after a while*) Ah, there's one now.
Annie Where?
John Hush, or he will bury himself in the mud. (*He makes as if to spear the fish*) Curses on it. It was but a grey pebble.
Annie Oh John, we had best go home. We must have gone two miles now, and you have not left a stone unturned.
John (*determinedly*) Mother shall have her loaches if it kills me.
Annie It might at that. Your poor feet must be frozen. Mine are with shoes and stockings on.
John You go back, Annie. Take the basket with the minnows. I shall go on up to Bagworthy water. There must be loaches there.
Annie No, John, it is too risky. Remember the Bagworthy stream runs out of Doone Valley. No-one ever ventures up there.
John Then there will be all the more loaches. Go on, sister. And make some good excuse why I am late.
Annie (*putting his shoes and socks into the bag*) Here, put your shoes and hose around your neck. And take Betty's breadcrust.

John takes them. Annie lingers

John Off you go then.
Annie Be careful, John. I have already lost a father. I have no wish to lose my brother too.

Annie goes out

We hear a sheepdog barking off. John puts the shoes round his neck, then starts to make his way up the stream

John (*as Narrator*) So I started to make my way up Bagworthy water where no grown man durst go. (*Beat*) Although I was frightened often by the deep dark places, I found it was a comely spot for catching loaches.

The boy John harpoons a loach and puts it in his bag

Then gradually the day began to fall behind the hilltops, and the cold grew worse and worse.

The Lights fade. John rubs his feet and legs before going on

And so, in a sorry plight, I came to an opening in the bushes and saw in front of me a great black pool.

The sound of the waterfall is heard as John reacts to the pool

I shuddered and drew back. Not only at the pool itself and the black air about it, but also at the whirling water and the strange roaring sound which came from the far end.

The roaring water sound peaks as John skirts round the pool

Skirting round, with very little comfort, for the rocks were high and steep, I saw, suddenly, the cause of the stir and roar. (*Beat*) For lo, between two cliffs, was a huge waterfall.

Lights create the waterfall

And now I was filled with a burning desire to climb the silvery slide and to discover what there was at the top. (*Beat*) Without stopping to look, for fear of my fear, I let my feet into the dip and rush of the torrent, and started to make my ascent.

We see the boy John's perilous ascent accompanied by suitably dramatic music and the crash of the waterfall. At one point he slips and almost falls into the pool, but somehow clings on and reaches the bright light at the top of the fall. Having done so, he loses his balance and, with a cry, plunges down into whatever lies beyond

Scene 6

A Meadow. Doone Valley

Sound of a stream. Birdsong

John lies unconscious

A little girl approaches. She is wearing a rich-coloured dress and has a shower of dark hair. She is Lorna Doone, aged nine. She is picking flowers. She stops with a gasp as she sees John

Lorna (*kneeling*) Wake up, boy. Oh, please wake up. (*She runs to the stream and damps a dainty handkerchief, then returns and wipes his brow with it*)

John groans as he regains consciousness

Oh, good, you are better. I am so glad.

John sits up, gazing at her with incredulity

I found you lying there. To begin with I thought you were dead.
John So did I. And that you were an angel!
Lorna (*laughing delightedly*) Who are you? How did you come here? And what are these wet things in your bag?
John (*pulling them away from her*) Leave them alone if you please. They are loaches for my mother. (*He sees her hurt expression*) But I will give you some, if you like.
Lorna Is your mother very poor? Yes, she must be. You have no shoes or stockings.
John She is not! Why we are rich enough to buy all this meadow if we choose. (*He takes out his shoes and hose*) And here are my shoes and hose.
Lorna Oh, they are as wet as your poor feet. (*She looks at his feet closer*) And see how they bleed! Will you let me bathe them?
John No!
Lorna (*misunderstanding*) I will do it very gently.
John (*awkwardly*) It is not for you to tend my feet.
Lorna Let me, please. (*She runs to the stream, dips her hanky in it, returns and starts to bathe John's feet*)

He looks at her with disbelief

Why do you look at me so?

John I never saw anyone like you before.
Lorna Nor I you! What is your name?
John John Ridd. What is yours?
Lorna (*hanging her head*) I cannot tell you.
John Why not?
Lorna Because if I do you will not like me.
John (*grinning*) No name can be that bad.
Lorna Oh, it can.
John Tell me.
Lorna It is ... Lorna Doone.
John (*duly shaken*) You are a Doone?
Lorna Yes. (*She starts to cry*) I knew you would not like me.
John (*going to her*) I like you very much indeed. Don't cry. Whatever your kinfolk may have done, I am sure you have never harmed anyone. See, Lorna, I will give you all my fish and catch some more for Mother.

Lorna flings her arms round him, still crying. He pushes her hair back from her face

Oh, please don't cry. (*He kisses her gently*)

She touches her cheek, then runs down to the stream embarrassed. John packs up his things, cross with himself and her. He makes a show of it

Very well. I will be off now. (*Getting no response, he looks up wondering how he will get out of the valley. Then he looks back at Lorna. He goes to her*) Lorna?
Lorna I thought you were going.
John Don't be angry with me. I did not mean to kiss you. I hate kissing. Ask my sisters.
Lorna I am not angry. Only frightened. Do you know what they would do if they found you here?
John Beat me I daresay.
Lorna No, they would kill you.
John Why should they kill me?
Lorna Because you have found the way up here. Now please go, oh please, John. And never come back.

He makes to protest

Well, perhaps just once to tell me if your feet are better. (*Quickly*) No, not even that!
John Yes, I shall. I shall come back often.

Act I, Scene 6   19

Lorna No, you must not!
John And I shall bring you all sorts of things. There are apples still and a thrush I found with only one leg, and our dog has just had puppies.
Lorna (*excitedly*) A puppy?
John I will bring you the best of the litter.
Lorna (*unhappily again*) No, they would never let me have a dog. Go please. (*She holds out her hand formally*) Goodbye, John Ridd.
John (*taking her hand*) How small your hand is.
Lorna You must not come back again. Ever.

A beat. Suddenly, a shout echoes down the valley

Carver (*off*) Lorna! Lorna!
Lorna (*gasping in horror*) They are looking for me!
John Come with me back down the waterfall. My mother will take care of you.
Lorna I cannot. Quick, go before they find us. See that gap in the rock there. (*She indicates the narrow gap*) There is a way out from the top of it. They would kill me if they knew I'd told you.
Carver (*off; nearer*) Lorna? Where are you?
Charlie (*off*) Lorna!
Lorna (*pushing John towards the gap*) They're coming. Quick. And never come back here again. You must forget you ever saw me.
John I shall never do that. (*He climbs into the gap but does not leave*)

Lorna hurries away as Carver and Charlie continue to call her. She lies down by the stream and pretends to be asleep

Carver enters, followed by Charlie, who carries a bottle of liquor

Carver Lorna? (*He sees her*) Here she is, our little princess. Fast asleep, by God.
Charlie (*looking down at her*) How fair she is.
Carver Nothing to what she'll be when she is full grown.
Charlie I will carry her back.
Carver No, Charlie, you will not. I have first claim on her. (*He picks her up*) Haven't I, Lorna? And no-one else shall touch her.

John almost comes out of his retreat so incensed is he

Come, my little princess, let's take you home.

Carver exits, carrying Lorna, followed by Charlie

John steps out of the niche in the rock and watches them go

John I shall return. One day.

He turns and goes into the niche

SCENE 7

Plovers' Barrows' Farm. A few months later. Summer 1674

Sarah is busy in the kitchen. Lizzie sits reading

After a moment, Annie comes running into the yard, breathless and excited

Annie Mother! Mother! Lizzie! Mother!
Sarah (*coming into the yard, followed by Lizzie*) What is it, Annie?
Annie There is a gentleman coming and he saved one of the ducks and then John asked if he could ride his horse and——
Sarah Now what is all this blather? Take a deep breath and tell me slowly.
Annie Well the ducks were making a terrible quacking so I went to see what ailed them, and I found the old white drake was missing. John and I searched and we found him in the brook. The torrent had washed him out and he was jammed in the floodwood. John was about to rush in after him—and I was afraid he would drown too so great was the swell—when this horseman called out to us. Then into the water he rode and rescued the old drake and gave him two peppercorns from his waistcoat till he flapped his wings and waddled off. The drake that is to say. And Mother, d'you know what? He says he is a cousin of Father's!
Sarah And what, pray, is the name of this gentleman?
Annie He is Master Faggus.
Sarah Faggus? That is no gentleman. That is a roysting drunken robber.
Lizzie (*excitedly*) You mean *Tom* Faggus the highwayman?
Sarah Whose worthless neck your father saved on more than one occasion.
Lizzie Then the horse must be Winnie, his famous mare. Folk say she is a witch!
Annie Even if he is a highwayman, he cannot be a wicked man. Not wicked like the Doones.
Lizzie They say he never robs a *poor* man, nor sheds a drop of blood. *And* he gives to the church.
Sarah Where do you learn such things, Lizzie?
Lizzie I keep my ears open.
Annie I am sure there is no bad in Master Faggus, Mother. Nor in his horse. Although she threw John off her back she——

Act I, Scene 7

Sarah Threw him, did you say?
Annie Yes, but when he fell, she nuzzled him most gently.
Sarah That may be, but...

She breaks off as she hears the sound of laughter off

Lizzie Here they come.

Tom Faggus enters with John. He leads his beautiful strawberry mare. Tom is somewhere between twenty-five and thirty. He is a wiry man of medium height with a ruddy complexion and a watchful eye. He has a flamboyant personality and great charm. John looks dishevelled, his jacket muddy and torn

It is obvious that Annie has fallen for Tom. During the following, Lizzie will eye Winnie curiously

Tom (*approaching*) No, you did well, lad! We may teach you to ride yet. I didn't think to see you stick on so long.
John I should have stuck on longer, sir, if her sides had not been wet. She was so slippery.
Tom (*laughing*) You are right, boy. She has given many the slip! Haven't you, my Winnie mare? (*He sees Sarah and Lizzie*) Why bless my soul, I do see my cousin Sarah, and young Lizzie I'll be bound.
Sarah No, you do see a mother distracted. What have you done to my boy?
John It's all right, Mother. I just took a tumble.
Sarah Foul shame on you, Tom Faggus, to put a young boy on that ugly beast.
Annie She is not ugly, she is beautiful.
Tom (*chucking her chin*) As you are, little Annie.
Sarah Fie upon you, Tom Faggus. Would you try to kill my son after all his father did for you? And if that animal comes into our yard I'll hamstring it myself.
John No, Mother. Winnie shall stop here the night or I will go away with her. I knew not what it was till now to ride a horse worth riding.
Tom (*acting up*) Thank you, John, but I had best not tarry. I see I am nothing here since I lost my poor cousin Ridd.
Sarah He was only a *distant* cousin.
Tom Close enough to have promised my dying mother he would take good care of me. Ah, there was a man! I may be a bad one myself in some ways, but I know the value of a good one. By God, if I could strike down those Doones!
Sarah We need not your aid, Tom Faggus. God will punish them.

John (*thinking of Lorna*) And all the Doones may not be bad.
Tom Spoken like your Christian father. He would have been proud of you, lad. As your mother must be. And she need have no fear. As if I would let a son of John Ridd's mount my mare, had I not seen *his* courage in your eyes.
Sarah You had little thought for his jacket.
Tom (*heavily*) Well, I will be on my way since I am not wanted here.
Annie Oh, can they not stay for supper, Mother? Master Faggus must be hungry.
Tom No, Annie, bless your kind heart. I will not stay where I am not welcome. I own I had hoped for some victuals. (*He lays it on*) I have not tasted a crust since this time yesterday. I gave my meat to a poor widow. But I will go starve on the moor sooner than eat the best supper that ever was cooked in a place that is ashamed of me. (*He turns to go*) Come Winnie. Open the gate if you will, Cousin John.
Sarah No, stop, Cousin!

Tom stops

You had best stay the night. It would be unkinsmanlike to turn you away. Come Annie, help me prepare the food. John, you show Cousin Tom where to stable that creature.

She and Annie go into the house. Lizzie lingers looking at the horse

John This way, Master Faggus.

Tom stops, noticing Lizzie

Lizzie Is she a witch?
Tom If she is, Lizzie, she is a good witch who has saved my life on more than one occasion.

Lizzie and Tom stroke the horse

And if you ask her very sweetly, she will make all your dreams come true.

Adult John appears high up above Doone Valley

John (*as Narrator*) The years passed by, and I grew from a boy to a man. And my thoughts returned often to the fair child, Lorna Doone, and the touch of her soft little hand. (*Beat*) And so on the high day of St Valentine — when all maids are full of lovers — I went back up the Bagworthy stream

Act I, Scene 8

to the black whirlpool. I climbed again the waterfall and made my way down to the valley below. (*He descends into the valley*) Then, hiding behind a bush, I waited. Knowing in my heart that she would surely come.

SCENE 8

A meadow and Lorna's Bower. Doone Valley. February 1683

Only the sound of birdsong and the rippling of the stream is heard

John hides behind a bush. Then suddenly he hears the sound of a young woman singing sweetly in the distance

Lorna (*off; singing*)　　Love as if there be one
　　　　　　　　　　　　Come my love to be,
　　　　　　　　　　　　My love is for the one
　　　　　　　　　　　　Loving unto me.

John reacts

　　　　　　　　　　　　Not for me the show, love,
　　　　　　　　　　　　Of a gilded bliss,
　　　　　　　　　　　　Only thou must know, love.
　　　　　　　　　　　　What my value is.

Lorna appears. She has more than fulfilled her early promise of beauty. She carries a bunch of early primroses as she sings on, oblivious of John's presence

　　　　　　　　　　　　If in all the earth, love,
　　　　　　　　　　　　Thou hast none but me,
　　　　　　　　　　　　This shall be my worth, love
　　　　　　　　　　　　To be cheap to thee.

John steps out of his hiding place

　　　　　　　　　　　　But if so thou ever
　　　　　　　　　　　　Strivest to be——

She breaks off with a gasp as she sees him, then turns to run away

John　No, Lorna! Wait!

She stops

Do you not know me?
Lorna Who are you, sir? And how do you know my name?
John I am John Ridd. The boy who came to Glen Doone when you were but a little thing so high.
Lorna (*with ill-concealed delight*) The poor boy who gave me his fish!
John And whose life you saved by your quickness.
Lorna Oh yes, I remember it all. (*She restrains herself*) But you, Master Ridd, seem to have forgotten the dangers of this place.
John Indeed I have not. And greatly frightened I am of them when I am not looking at *you*.

Lorna looks down, not knowing what to say

See, I have brought you a present.

She looks up

Some new-laid eggs. Our young blue hen has just come into laying.
Lorna But how did you know you would find me?
John (*simply*) I just did. (*After a pause, he moves to a mossy tree trunk*) Let me lay them out for you. I would have brought you twice as many but I feared to crush them. (*He kneels, takes the eggs out of his pocket very carefully, one by one, and puts them down on the mossy "table", wiping the wisps of hay from each one*)

Lorna watches him, then suddenly stifles a sob. He looks up and sees her wiping her eyes with a handkerchief

(*Going to her*) What have I done? Tell me what I have done to make you weep.
Lorna It is nothing done by you. The scent of clover hay always affects me so. (*Beat*) Moreover I am not used to kindness.
John Next time I shall bring you some trout from our brook.
Lorna No, you must not come again. And you should leave now if you care for your life. The patrol will be here in a moment.
John I will not stir one step till I have spoken more with you.
Lorna (*after a moment's hesitation*) Well then be quick and follow me. I have a secret chamber in the upper valley. Come, Master Ridd.
John Not unless you call me John.
Lorna John then. Be quick. I hear them coming.

We hear voices off

Act I, Scene 8

Lorna and John exit quickly up a hidden path

Carver and Charlie approach from the back of the auditorium. Charlie now wears a beard and Carver appears even more formidable. They both carry guns

Carver There's no-one here.

A single birdsong is heard above the rest

It must have been that bird we heard. (*He aims his gun at the bird and shoots at it*)

The birdsong stops. He goes to pick up the bird. As he does so, he notices the eggs laid out on the mossy ledge

It looks as if a larger bird has been here. What is this? Is someone paying court to Lorna? (*Menacingly*) Is it you, Charlie? I've seen you looking at her. Is it? If so, by God, I'll — —
Charlie No, Carver. I swear it.
Carver Wait till I find out who it is. I shall roast him alive. (*He picks up a stone, holds it for a moment, then brings it down smashing the eggs*)

Black-out

Bring up the Lights on Lorna's bower. It is a natural room carved out of unhewn rock, decorated with a variety of fern and moss. The floor is soft grass. The ceiling is the sky, from which the light comes. The narrow entrance is covered with a sweep of ivy. The chairs are two large stones

Lorna draws the ivy aside as she shows John in

Lorna Mind your head.

John stoops to enter the room feeling large and gauche. He straightens himself up tentatively

(*Amused*) It's all right. The ceiling is the sky.

John looks round

Do you like it?
John Very much.

Lorna We should be safe from interruption now. None trespass on me here, except my little maid, Gwenny Carfax, who is the only person that I trust. Please be seated, Master... John.

They both sit. A pause

I never thought to entertain you here.

John There are so many things I want to ask you. How came you here? Who are your parents?

Lorna Would that I knew all the answers myself. If I ask those around me, I meet only with anger.

John Is there no one you can talk to?

Lorna Only my grandfather, Sir Ensor Doone. And he seems unwilling to ponder these matters.

John (*duly impressed*) Sir Ensor is your grandfather?

Lorna He would have me call him so. They say my father was his eldest son, long dead. But I cannot remember him, nor my mother. And yet — sometimes — I...

John What?

Lorna Sometimes I feel as if — as if there were some distant memory locked in the depth of my mind. A coach driving through the mist, people shouting... I reach out as if to grasp it and then a huge black wave comes crashing down sweeping away all recollection. (*She smiles embarrassedly*) Perhaps one day I will remember.

John Is it because of Sir Ensor that they call you their "princess"?

Lorna Princess and heiress to this dark realm. I sometimes wonder why they treat me with such deference. It is not likely that I, a woman, will hold much power or authority. Yet the Counsellor — our Judge and Treasurer — is respectful always. And his son, Carver, seeks my hand as if it were a royal alliance.

John (*shaken*) Carver? The Counsellor's son is Carver Doone?

Lorna I see that you have heard of him.

John I have heard of him right enough. It was he who killed my father.

Lorna Oh no, John, no!

John (*trying to restrain his emotion*) And this Carver — seeks your hand?

Lorna Yes, but I do not wish it so. I could not marry such a man. Apart from his wildness, he is thrice as old as I, and has other women and — —

John Lorna, you must leave this place at once. Come with me now.

Lorna I cannot. I must stay here as long as my grandfather lives.

John makes to interrupt

No, please! I could not bear that he should die and have no gentle hand to comfort him.

Act I, Scene 9

John (*restraining himself again*) Then may I come and visit you again?

She hesitates

> Say "yes".
>
> **Lorna** Yes. But not for a month at least.
> **John** A *month*?
> **Lorna** Sooner would be too dangerous.
> **John** What if you have need of me meantime? Can you not show me by some sign?
> **Lorna** Let me think. I know! Gwenny is allowed outside the valley to visit her aunt. If I am in danger I will tell her to throw a dark mantle over a big white rock which I will show you. It cannot be seen from inside the valley, but you will be able to spy it from the top.
> **John** (*taking her hand*) Promise you will do so. Whenever you should need me.
> **Lorna** I promise.

Scene 9

Plovers' Barrows' Farm. Three weeks later. Early evening

We see Jem Fry and the other labourers packing up and setting off home. They call "good-night" to each other

A pause. Then the sound of a horse neighing off

Jeremy (*off; calling*) Halloa!

Jeremy Stickles approaches from some way off. He is a tubby man in his forties, dressed in a well-cut, albeit muddy, riding suit. He walks with some difficulty having been in the saddle for some days. He is in a bad temper

(*Waving a parchment*) Halloa! You there!

John approaches from another direction

John Are you talking to me, sir?
Jeremy Who else would I be talking to? Come here, you great yokel, at risk of fine and imprisonment. I am in service of the King.

John walks towards him, taking his time

Make haste, I have not all night. Is there anywhere in this cursed county a place called Plovers' Barrows' Farm? *(Before John can answer)* And do not tell me "half an hour further" or "just round the corner". They have been telling me that for the last twenty miles. Well, do not stand there looking at me, bumpkin! Where is this cursed farm?

John This is Plovers' Barrows' Farm, sir.

Jeremy Thank the good Lord.

John And you are kindly welcome, sir. As are all visitors. Stay for supper if you will. We have sheep's kidneys.

Jeremy *(won over at once)* Sheep's kidneys?

John But why think you so badly of us? We do not like to be cursed so.

Jeremy Nay, young man, I think not badly of you. Nor of sheep's kidneys. They sound uncommon good. I have been in the saddle ten days, and never a comely meal. When people hear King's service cried they give me the worst of everything.

John You will not receive such treatment here. I am a thorough-going Church and State man and a Royalist.

Jeremy I am glad to hear it. There was not a house on the road would entertain me.

John *(calling)* Annie! Annie! My sister will see to your comfort, sir.

Annie, now eighteen, comes out of the farmhouse

Annie Did you call, brother?

John There is a gentleman come to sup. Bring down the cut ham.

Jeremy *(his mouth watering still more)* Cut ham did you say?

John And slice a few rashers of the hung deer's meat.

Jeremy Deer's meat?

Annie Right away.

Annie hurries off

Jeremy May I leave my horse in your hands? He is tethered up yonder and greatly foundered as am I.

John I will see to him directly, sir. Follow me if you will.

Jeremy *(following him)* Deer's meat... You are the right sort of folk and no mistake.

John leads Jeremy Stickles into the kitchen where the women are in a flurry of preparation. Sarah has aged beyond her forty years. Lizzie is now fifteen

John Here is our guest. He comes on King's service. *(To Jeremy)* My mother and my sisters.

Act I, Scene 9   29

They curtsy to him

Jeremy (*to Sarah*) Madam. My name is Jeremy Stickles. I am a servant of the King's Bench.
Sarah Be seated, sir, and rest yourself.
John Bring Master Stickles some ale, Lizzie, and fetch the hops out of the tap with a skewer that it may run more sparkling.
Jeremy All this shall go greatly in your favour, lad, when I make my report. But wait! I almost forgot the purpose of my visit.

Lizzie stops in her tracks to listen

I must speak to one John Ridd. I beg you tell me he is close at hand or I must eat my saddle.
John No need for that, sir. I am John Ridd.
Jeremy God be praised. Then, in the name of the King, His Majesty Charles the Second, receive this, Master Ridd. (*He hands him the rolled parchment*)

It is tied across and waxed. John opens it slowly. The others watch

Pray read it quickly, lad, or my supper will spoil.
Lizzie Go on, John.
Sarah What is it, John? What does it say?
John (*reading*) "To our good subject, John Ridd. Greeting. You are required, in the name of our Lord the King, to appear in person before the Right Worshipful, the Justices of His Majesty's Bench at Westminster— —"
Lizzie Westminster!
John "—to give evidence about certain matters whereby the peace of our said Lord and the well-being of his realm may be imperilled."
Sarah He is to go to London?
Jeremy At once. Putting aside all else. Charges will be borne. Now if I might have that ale?
John (*thinking of Lorna*) When must we leave?
Jeremy First thing tomorrow. I will need a fresh horse.
John Tomorrow? But I cannot leave so soon. I must go to… That is, I have important matters to attend to here.
Jeremy King's orders.
John Could His Majesty's business not save another week?
Jeremy Certainly not. Nor even another day!
Annie (*deliberately*) What a shame. We have a yearling turkey that would roast well in a day or two.
John That's right, Annie.
Jeremy (*tempted*) Turkey?

Annie And one of our young suckling pigs would make a good meal for Saturday. Isn't that so, John?

John Why yes, there be too many for the sow, so one could go for roasting.

Jeremy Well perhaps... No! My journey has taken too long already due to the uncivil treatment I met on the way. If we delay further we will meet the King's displeasure.

John Surely just one day more——

Jeremy We leave tomorrow and no further argument. Where is that ale?

John Fetch the ale, Lizzie, while I go tend to Master Stickles' horse. (*He goes out quickly*)

Annie Wait, John!

John Oh Annie, what am I to do?

Annie You are troubled about Lorna Doo——

John Hush! Do not speak her name. No one but you must know. I promised I would visit her after a month. What will she think if I do not arrive? And what if she signals that something is wrong?

Annie You cannot disobey the King or it will mean trouble for us all.

John Oh, pray no harm befalls her while I am gone.

Annie (*helping him into a jacket for London*) And pray no harm befalls *you* on the journey to London. It is a long and dangerous route, and Master Stickles will receive no hospitality bearing the badge of the King.

John Then I shall tell all the inn-keepers that Tom Faggus is my cousin.

Annie Oh yes! There is not a house on the road but should not be proud to entertain *him*.

John Would that I had his magic horse too, that I might return more quickly to Lorna. (*He steps forward as Narrator*) So off we set the following morn, and due to Tom Faggus's pass we arrived in London, ten days later, in excellent condition.

The Lights dim

The night was falling very thick as we came to Tyburn. Master Stickles thought it wise for us to halt there because the way was unsafe by night across Charing village. I was for my part nothing loath, preferring to see London by daylight.

Bring in London noises and bring up the Lights

But after all it was nothing worth seeing. A very hideous and dirty place, not at all like Exmoor.

A clerk comes in with a document for John to sign

The day after we arrived I was delivered up to the Chief Clerk. Where I signed a deed agreeing that, on pain of a heavy fine, I would hold myself ready and present to give evidence when called upon. (*He sighs*) The Law! I had heard of its delays but never thought to have such bitter experience of the evil myself. Master Stickles had left on other business so I had no-one to aid me. (*He wends his way through a chain of clerks*) I traipsed from Inn to Inn and clerk to clerk. But all to no avail. And all the while my thoughts were with Lorna and the perils that might assail her in my absence.

Spotlight on the white rock, high up, as Gwenny Carfax, a very small and stout woman of indeterminate age, covers it with a dark mantle

(*Determinedly*) At length I determined to listen to clerks no more, but to force my way up to the Lord Chief Justice. Though my heart was in my hose. For I had heard of the reputation of the dread Judge Jeffreys.

Scene 10

Judge Jeffreys' Chamber. Summer 1683

Spank, a clerk, leads John Ridd down the corridor towards Judge Jeffreys' chamber

Spank (*pausing as they reach the door*) A word of advice, young man, before you have your audience with Judge Jeffreys. Doubtless you have heard of his reputation?
John Yes, sir.
Spank They do not call him the Hanging Judge for nothing. When His Lordship cross-examines you, answer the truth at once, else he will have it out of you by other means.
John Yes, sir.
Spank And mind he likes not to be contradicted, and never make him speak twice.
John No, sir.
Spank Oh, and should he make some jest, which he is wont to do, be sure to laugh most heartily.
John Thank you, Master Spank. I am obliged to you.

Spank knocks on the door. A voice barks at him to enter. He does so. John follows

Judge Jeffreys is busy with some papers. He is a stout man whose moods can change in a second

Spank May it please Your Worship——
Judge What is it, Spank?
Spank John Ridd, my lord.

John comes in

Spank exits

John Your Worship. (*He bows*)

Judge Jeffreys continues to peruse his papers. John shifts awkwardly. After a while, the Judge looks up at him

Judge What name did Spank say?
John John Ridd, sir.
Judge Who are you and why are you here? Answer, John Ridd, or I shall soon be *rid* of you.

John, thinking this to be a joke, laughs

(*Sharply*) Why do you laugh?
John I laugh at your wit, sir.
Judge Then you are not as *half*-witted as you look. (*He laughs*)

John joins in. The Judge stops laughing abruptly

So, give me your credentials and be quick about it.
John (*taking a deep breath*) I am of Oare Parish, sir, in the county of Somerset, brought to London some two months ago by a special messenger called Jeremy Stickles and bound over to be ready to be called upon to give evidence in a matter unknown to me, but touching the peace of our Lord the King and the welfare of his subjects. And every day, save Sunday, I have walked up and down the Great Hall of Westminster, expecting to be called upon, yet no one has called me, and now I desire to ask Your Worship whether I may go home again for I am needed there right urgently. (*He finishes, panting*)

Judge Jeffreys laughs

Judge I wager you have never made so long a speech before.
John No, sir.
Judge And you are a spunky lad to make it now. I recall the matter. (*He opens a file*) You have been waiting two months you say.
John Nearer three now, sir.

Act I, Scene 10 33

Judge I grieve for His Majesty's exchequer, keeping you all that time.
John Nay, my lord, it is my mother has been keeping me. Not a groat have I received from the exchequer.
Judge (*erupting in sudden fury*) What? This is an outrage. (*He calls*) Spank! Spank!

Spank scuttles in

Spank You called, Your Worship?
Judge John Ridd maintains he has received no monies yet. Is His Majesty come to this? That he starves his own supporters?
Spank (*stuttering*) My lord, I—I— —
Judge Is this true?
Spank Yes, Your Worship, but— —
Judge You mean this young man has been dragged from his home and adoring mother at the height of agriculture at his own cost and charge?
Spank So it would seem, sir, but— —
Judge You have swindled the money yourself, foul Spank. Yes, that is it!
Spank No, Your Worship. The thing has been overlooked with so many grave acts of treason.
Judge As I will *overlook* your head on a spike from Temple Bar if ever I hear the like again.
Spank But sir, I— —
Judge Answer me not. Go see to it. One more word and I will have you on a hurdle.

Spank hurries out

(*Subsiding as quickly as he erupted*) The matter will be dealt with.
John Thank you, sir.
Judge (*staring hard at him*) To be sure you are a hefty lad.
John I reckon I have lost weight fretting so long here in London.
Judge And there is much fret in you to lose! Now John—or methinks by the look of you you are more used to being called "Jack".
John Yes, sir. But only by old Betty Muxworthy.
Judge Peace you forward varlet! There is a deal too much of you. We shall have to try short commons with you, and you are a very long common. (*He laughs*) Ha ha! Spank must hear that by and by. It is beyond your thick head.
John Not so, my lord. I was at Blundell's School, and there I heard many bad jokes.

For a minute we think the Judge is going to erupt in anger, but then he laughs loudly

Judge Ha, ha! That hit you hard, did it? And faith it would be hard to miss you, even with a harpoon! Now Jack Whale, having hauled you hard, I will proceed to examine you.

John I am ready to answer, my lord.

Judge (*consulting papers*) Tell me, is there in your part of the world a certain band of robbers and outlaws whom all men fear to handle?

John Yes, my lord. At least some of them are robbers, and all are outlaws.

Judge And what is your High Sheriff about that he does not hang them all, or send them up for me to hang?

John I reckon that he is afraid, my lord. Their valley is well-guarded, and then they are of good birth.

Judge Good birth! 'Tis the surest way to the block to be a chip off the old one. (*He laughs*) What is the name of the pestilent race and how many are there?

John They are the Doones of Bagworthy Forest. And there are about forty of them, beside the women and children.

Judge Forty Doones, all forty thieves! How long have they been there?

John About thirty years, my lord. Maybe forty. They came before the great war broke out. Some quarrel over land I believe. But 'tis longer back than I remember.

Judge Good, you speak plainly. Woe betide a liar when I get hold of him. And now to another matter. Have you heard of a man called Tom Faggus?

John Why yes, sir. He is my own cousin and I fear...

Judge (*sharply*) What do you fear?

John That he is overfond of my sister Annie.

Judge (*laughing*) She could do far worse. Tom Faggus has made mistakes and I fear he will come to the gallows, but he shall never be condemned by me. Now one thing more. Is there any sign around your way of disaffection to His Majesty?

John No, my lord. No sign that I know of. We pray for him in church, but after that we have nothing more to say about him.

Judge Hm. The less you say the better. But I have heard of treacherous talk and deeds in Tiverton. Of plans afoot to bring back the traitor Monmouth.

John (*with disbelief*) In Tiverton?

Judge And even nearer you in Dulverton.

John Not Dulverton, sir!

Judge I see that you know nothing of all that. Keep clear of it, John. It will come to nothing. I shall see to that. But many shall swing for it. (*He looks back at the papers*) Begone now. I had thought to use you as a spy but see you are too honest for the job. I will remember you, and think that you will not forget me either.

John No, sir. (*He bows*)

John leaves

Judge (*as John goes*) And keep away from those Doones too. (*He calls*) Spank!

Spank hurries in

Spank Yes, Your Worship?
Judge I will now attend to the matter of Master Algernon Sidney. (*Pointedly*) We will soon make *republic* of him, for his state shall shortly be headless!
Spank Headless! Very good, sir!

They laugh uproariously

John (*as Narrator*) Much as I longed to go at once to Lorna, and though my heart was yearning, I could not leave my family on the very minute of my arrival home. But the very next day I took my chance and before long I stood at the head of the slippery waterfall, gazing into Doone Valley.

Scene 11

A meadow. Doone Valley. Lorna's Bower

John looks around hoping to see Lorna

Gwenny Carfax comes up behind him

Gwenny Oy!

John turns quickly. For a minute he does not notice her as she is so much smaller than he is

Be you Master Ridd?
John I am.
Gwenny Whoy! Aren't you big? Big as any Doone I do swear.
John You must be Gwenny.
Gwenny So I am. You took your time a-comin'. It be two month since I threw the mantle over yon white stone for a signal.
John (*urgently*) Is she safe?
Gwenny No thanks to you. Come on then! Don't just stand there. She's up there in her chamber. You go to her, and I will wait and watch out for 'ee.

John hurries off

Gwenny positions herself to keep watch

Bring up the Lights on Lorna's bower; the flowers and leaves are now those of summer

Lorna sits sewing

John enters quietly through the ivy covered entrance

She does not see him

John (*after a beat*) Lorna?
Lorna (*turning*) John!
John I thought you might have need of me.
Lorna I did, but that was weeks ago, and you did not come.
John Do not be vexed. I was called to London on King's business. They kept me there for over three months. There was no way I could let you know.
Lorna I thought you had forgotten me.
John Forget you? Never! (*He restrains himself*) Why did you signal for me?
Lorna They tried to make me swear that I would wed Carver.
John (*beside himself*) Wed him? When? Tell me!
Lorna (*calming him*) Oh, not at once. I am still too young. But they wanted me to be formally betrothed to him in the presence of my grandfather. It was at Carver's insistence and Counsellor's too.
John Why now?
Lorna There is a Doone called Charlewood. We know him as Charlie. They fancy that he looks at me too much when he passes my grandfather's cottage.
John (*heatedly*) He had better not! Or I will fling this Charlie over the roof.
Lorna (*laughing in spite of herself*) Oh John, you are worse than Carver! And I thought you were so kind and gentle.
John How did you answer them?
Lorna I refused to swear their oath. Carver wanted to use force on me.
John The fiend!
Lorna But my grandfather would not hear of it.
John Oh Lorna, if only I had been there.
Lorna And now I am watched and spied and followed. I would not be speaking with you now but for my dear Gwenny.
John Do not fear. I shall make sure that none ever wed you but I!

She looks at him startled. He realises what he has said

> You must know of my feelings for you. I love you, Lorna, and *have* done ever since I first saw you as a little girl. Tell me you love me too.

Act I, Scene 11

Lorna I like you very much.
John But do you love me?
Lorna I think of you almost every day.
John *Almost* will not do! I think of you every instant. For you I would give up my home, my life, my hope of life beyond it!
Lorna You talk so wildly!
John Then say you love me too.

She hesitates

I know you are far above me in birth and education, and that there is no reason why someone as beautiful as you should love a common yeoman who— —
Lorna Hush! Speak not of yourself so! Of course I love you.
John Oh Lorna... (*He takes her into his arms*)
Lorna But I fear the danger that my love may bring you. Perhaps one day you will be sorry to be loved by such as I.
John Rather would I be sorry to have *lived*.

They embrace

Oh Lorna, my dearest love. (*Then he remembers*) Look, I have bought you something in London. (*He takes out a ring*)
Lorna A ring! It is beautiful.

He goes to put it on her finger

But no, John! I dare not take it now, else I should be cheating you. I hope in time I will be able to love you as you wish and deserve. Keep it for me till then.

John takes it and puts it close to his heart

John (*as Narrator*) I returned home on that bright summer's day with oh, such joy in my heart, for I knew for certain and forever, that Lorna Doone returned my love. (*Beat*) The weeks passed by and we did meet through the help of a mode of signals left in secret places by Gwenny Carfax.

Mist begins to roll in

The harvest came and went. Then the leaves did start to fall and dull autumn mists covered the tors. But though I visited Lorna's glen every day, I could find no sign of mistress or maid. (*Beat*) Desperate I was, knowing not if

Lorna was stolen, dangered, perhaps outraged. And so, one night, in spite of Annie's pleas, I resolved to penetrate Doone Valley itself.

The Lights dim as John moves off

Scene 12

Sir Ensor's House. Doone Valley. Night

It is dark and misty. Hazy moonlight and a faint gleam from the upper barred window of Sir Ensor's house. An owl hoots off

We see John creeping cautiously down the steep path. As he nears the bottom we hear Charlie's voice off

Charlie (*off*) Curse it, my flint is out. Give me the lantern and stay there.

John quickly conceals himself

Charlie approaches. As he passes Captain's house he looks up at the lighted window

Carver comes from his own house, carrying a lamp

Carver Who's there?

Charlie whistles a few notes of a distinctive tune to identify himself

Which of you is it?
Charlie 'Tis I, Carver, Charlie.
Carver You are supposed to be standing sentry, not prowling under Lorna's chamber.
Charlie I was not. It was you I was seeking.
Carver I hope so, Charlie, I hope so. For I will fling you senseless into the river if ever I catch you paying court to her.
Charlie Never fear. We all know she is to be yours. The rest of us must be content with coarser stuff than you would have.
Carver Would have? Ay, and *will* have. What do you want with me?
Charlie A light for my lantern. And a glass of schnapps if you have one.
Carver You have had enough already. I smell it on your breath. (*He kindles the lantern*) Here, take your light. And now be off with you before I punch your head into a new wick for your lantern.

Act I, Scene 12

Charlie Gladly. You are not pleasant company tonight.

Charlie goes and joins his fellow sentry

Carver pauses for a moment. He looks up at Lorna's window

Carver I bide my time, Princess, but not for long.

Carver goes back to his house

John comes out from his hiding place

John (*with emotion*) And not for long will I bide mine, Carver Doone! (*He crosses the bridge quietly, picks up a pebble and throws it at Lorna's window*)

No response. He throws another. The curtain over the window is drawn back

Lorna opens the rough lattice covering the bars. She is in night attire

(Sotto voce) Lorna?
Lorna (*nervously*) Who is it?
John Oh Lorna, don't you know me?
Lorna John! (*She puts her hand through the bars*) Oh John, you must be mad.
John Mad with worry having no news of you. You must have known I'd come.
Lorna Well, I thought—perhaps——
John Oh course you did. Oh Lorna! (*He kisses her hand*) These cursed bars. Why are they put up here? Has your grandfather turned against you?
Lorna No, but he is very ill. I fear that he will not live long. The Counsellor and Carver are masters here. Gwenny is not allowed to leave the valley any more, so I could send no message. I have been so wretched lest you should think me false. (*She gasps as a shadow crosses the moon*)
John 'Tis only a bat. Oh, my poor love, you are trembling so.
Lorna I am so frightened they will find you. I should die if they hurt you. Oh, go, go if you love me.
John How can I go without settling anything? How shall I know of your danger now? Think of something please.
Lorna There is a tree with seven rooks' nests against the cliffs at the far end of the valley. Can you count them from above, do you think? From a place you will be safe?
John No doubt of it.

Lorna Gwenny can climb like a cat. If you see but six nests I am in peril. If but five, Carver has carried me off.
John My God, if that should happen I— —
Lorna Hush! Fear not, my darling. (*Sombrely*) I have means to stop him, or at least to save myself. If you can come within a day you will find me quite unharmed. After that if *you* cannot have me, no one will.
John Oh Lorna, Lorna...
Charlie (*off*) I think I heard a voice. I had best go see.
Lorna Quick. Someone comes.
John God bless you, my love. (*He darts across the bridge*)

Charlie enters

Charlie Who's there?

John freezes. We see Charlie standing in the moonlight. His gun is trained on John whose outline is just visible through the mist

I said who's there? Answer or I will fire.

A beat, then John whistles the tune he heard Carver whistle earlier

Oh Carver, it is you. I thought you had gone to your house. (*He sees the light in Lorna's window*) Oho, I see what you are at. I will leave you to your courting. (*As he goes to join his mate*) It's all right. It was only Carver. Come on, let us have a game of push-pin.

Charlie goes

John steps forward and blows a kiss to Lorna which she returns. He hurries up the path

Lorna Oh John, who am I to dream of another life? Something in my heart tells me it can never be so.

Scene 13

The Seven Rooks' Nests. Winter

We see Gwenny climbing the rocks up to where the seven rooks' nests are. She is removing one when John hails her

John Gwenny!

Act I, Scene 14

Gwenny You nearly had me fall! Thank the Lord 'tis you.
John Only six nests! (*He joins her*) Is Lorna in danger?
Gwenny No, but you must come with me now.
John Why? What's happened?
Gwenny Old Sir Ensor be dying. And he cannot die, or at least he will not, without first seeing *you*.
John Has your mistress told him then? About——
Gwenny Your courtin' of her? Ay, she has, *and* your other doin's. I tried to stop her, but she would have her way. She said she could not deceive him at the end.
John (*with some trepidation*) What did he say?
Gwenny That vexed he was, I thought he would recover on purpose for to thrash 'ee. Fire I have seen before, hot and raging. But not cold fire like *his*. (*She shudders*) It made me fair shiver. I would not be in your boots, Master.
John I could wish for others.
Gwenny Why don't you give her up? No good can come of it.
John (*with fervour*) Because I love her, Gwenny. As you do, or you would not be here now.
Gwenny (*beat*) Come then, follow me. There is a short way through the thicket.

They go

Scene 14

Sir Ensor's House

Two Doones are lounging by the waterside

Gwenny approaches, followed by John

The Doones at once spring to their feet

Doone Who goes there?
Gwenny Never you mind. Sir Ensor has sent for him and ordered his protection.

The Doones lower their guns. They stare after John as he and Gwenny cross the bridge

Lorna opens the door

Lorna Oh John, I knew you'd come.

John and Lorna go inside. Gwenny plonks herself down outside the door

Gwenny (*to the Doones*) I know I be a thing of beauty, but there is no call to stand there staring at me.

John and Lorna go into Sir Ensor's room

> *He is sitting upright in the throne chair, a loose red cloak over him, his white hair falling on his shoulders, his face deathly pale*

Lorna Here he is, Grandfather.
Ensor Come here, John Ridd.

John goes to him, followed by Lorna who will stand beside Sir Ensor

(*Peering at him*) You are mightily grown since last we met.
John I did not think you would remember, sir.
Ensor Grown in height but not in sense. Do you realize what you are doing?
John Yes, sir.
Ensor That you have set your eyes far above your rank?
John I know of her descent from the Doones of Bagworthy.
Ensor And know you of your own descent from the Ridds of Oare?
John Sir, the Ridds of Oare have been honest men twice as long as the Doones have been rogues.
Ensor (*unexpectedly quiet*) I would not answer for that. But hearken to me, boy. And you too, Lorna. Hearken to an old man who has not long to live.
Lorna Oh no, Grandfather.
Ensor There is nothing in the world worth risking your life for. Least of all love. All marriage is a wretched farce. Even when the man and wife belong to the same rank. But when they are ill-matched as you, the farce becomes a long dull tragedy. Therefore I forbid you to see this foolish child again. You will pledge your word now in her presence.
John (*after a beat*) No, sir. I will never do that. I will pledge only to love and protect her as long as I may live.
Ensor (*shaken*) Lorna? What say you? You will not disobey me at my last hour?

Lorna hesitates, then goes quietly to John's side

(*With a deep weariness*) You two fools.
John May it please Your Worship, we are content to be fools as long as we may be fools together.

Lorna takes his arm

Act I, Scene 14

Ensor Such passion is more fit for southern climes than the fogs of Exmoor.
John And when it happens so, there is nothing can stop it. Or *no one*, Sir.
Lorna Please Grandfather, give us your blessing.
Ensor How can I bless a coupling that is cursed? (*He sinks back wearily*) Fools you are. Be fools forever. It is the best thing I can wish you. (*He turns and takes something out of a box beside him*) Lorna, take this. (*He hands her what appears to be a glass necklace*)
Lorna Why! It is the glass necklace I wore as a child! You took it for safe-keeping.
Ensor Take it now and keep it close to you.

She takes it. He sinks back in his chair

And leave me. I am weary...

Lorna stoops and kisses him gently. John bows. They go out, and stand at the door for a moment

John Lorna, come with me now.
Lorna I cannot. I could not bear him to die on his own, unloved by anyone.
John (*accepting with reluctance*) I will come again soon. Farewell, my love. (*He kisses her*)
Lorna Gwenny, go with him to Doone Gate. (*She goes back inside*)

John and Gwenny cross the bridge and come face to face with Carver. Counsellor follows behind

Carver And who might this be?
John I am John Ridd whose father you killed.
Carver Ah yes. I have heard of you. How came you here?
John Sir Ensor sent for me. I have told him that I love Lorna, as she does me.
Carver (*almost speechless*) What did you say?
John That I love Lorna and intend to have her for my wife.
Carver (*with a roar*) So it is you who has been courting her? (*He raises his gun*) Well, John Ridd, you will soon follow your father to— —
Counsellor No, Carver! (*He stops him*) Hold your fire! Have you no respect for the Captain? The quarrel will wait.
Carver (*slowly lowering his gun*) Go then. But remember, when the old man dies *I* shall be leader here, and Lorna Doone will be my queen!

CURTAIN

ENTR'ACTE

The Lights come up on John

John (*as Narrator*) Soon after my visit to Doone Valley Sir Ensor died. (*Beat*) Before he was buried, the greatest frost of the century set in. Three good pick-axes were broken ere the gravediggers could penetrate the hard earth. (*Beat*) Not a tear was shed for the old man save from Lorna's sweet eyes. Not a sigh pursued him home. Even the holy water froze upon his coffin. (*Beat*) And then came the snow...

Snow effect. During the following, we see some of the labourers shovelling snow. While, in the background, others struggle through the blizzard, a sheep under each arm. Plaintive bleating

It snowed and snowed, harder than it had ever snowed before. Great drifts rolled and curled in billows as high as a barn. (*Beat*) Although for people who had no sheep, the sight was a very fine one, yet for those with their flock underneath it, it had but little charm. (*With emotion*) And for those cut off entirely from their loved ones, still less cheer.

He goes into the farm kitchen

ACT II

Scene 1

Plovers' Barrows' Farm. January 1684

Snow all around. It is early morning

Annie is giving John his breakfast before he goes to work. They are both in low spirits

John If only there was some way I could reach Doone Valley. But I cannot even reach the high slopes to rescue our sheep.
Annie Lord knows when I shall see Tom again.
John (*emotionally*) At least he is not in danger from Carver Doone.

Act II, Scene 1

Annie (*her voice cracking*) But he may be in danger from hanging.
John (*putting his arm round her*) Oh Annie, I did not mean to hurt you. You are the only person I can talk to of Lorna.
Annie And I you, of Tom. I would tell Mother, but I know she will not let me wed him.
John Your news will be nothing to mine. Her only son in love with a Doone! Even though she be the sweetest, noblest maid who ever lived. Oh Annie, when I think that brute Carver may at this very instant be — —
Lizzie (*off*) John!
Annie Hush! Lizzie is coming! She must not know! (*Deliberately*) Eat up your breakfast now, John.

Lizzie comes in, carrying a book

Lizzie Ah John! Good. You are not yet gone out shovelling.
John Mistress Eliza! Up already? You are usually in your nightcap at this hour.
Lizzie I wanted to tell you something I read in this book.
John Reading! That's all you ever think of.
Lizzie It's a pity *you* never read. You might learn something.
John Reading won't save our sheep, will it?
Annie I've never known a winter like it. I almost froze in bed last night.
Lizzie The climate is ten times worse than this in the arctic regions of the far north. It never ceases to freeze and snow there, and no sun is up for months at a time.
John Not another lecture!
Lizzie (*pointedly*) Yet people manage to go about their daily business.
John (*going to fetch his sheepskin*) I have no time to listen. I have a hundred and one things to see to.
Lizzie You are an even greater fool than I thought, John Ridd.
John And you more full of airs and graces.
Annie Oh stop it, both of you!
Lizzie Well, I should have thought he would be right glad to learn how to get through the snow to Doone Valley.

Annie and John stop in their tracks

John (*trying to sound nonchalant*) Why on earth should I want to go to Doone Valley of all places?
Lizzie To see your beloved Lorna Doone, of course.

John's mouth drops open

You think I do not know? I have ears and eyes. And I have seen you going

about like a lovesick sheep for the past year or more. Why you must be as besotted with *her* as Annie is with our cousin Tom Faggus.
Annie (*reacting*) How did you...?
Lizzie You should hear yourself talk as you sleep. (*She imitates*) "Tom, darling Tom. When will you come to me?"
John Why didn't you tell us you knew?
Lizzie I know you two like to have your little secrets.
John (*anxiously*) Does Mother know?
Lizzie Oh, Mother doesn't notice anything. She still has Sally Rowe in mind for you. (*Deliberately*) Well, since you do not wish to learn how to cross the snow as Eskimos do— —
John (*stopping her*) No, Lizzie, wait! I am sorry if I spoke in haste. How *do* these Eskimos get along?
Lizzie (*taking her time*) With shoes like boats on either feet. (*Seeing she has their interest*) They are very strong but very light, and made with ribs with skin drawn across them. There is a diagram in my book.
John Show me.

Annie and John gather round as Lizzie shows the diagram

Lizzie There. See.

Sarah comes in unnoticed

Annie Oh John, do you think you could make some? Then you could skim across the moors to visit Lorna Doone.
Sarah Visit *who*?

They all turn to look at her, horrified

John (*after a beat*) You might as well know, Mother, for soon I shall bring her to you. I love Sir Ensor's granddaughter. Lorna Doone.
Sarah *What?*
Annie And *I* wish to marry Tom Faggus.

Sarah faints

The girls carry her off

John goes to pick up snow shoes to which he puts the finishing touches. He then puts them on proudly, takes a step, catches one shoe in the other and falls over. He gets up and tries again, more successfully

Act II, Scene 2

Scene 2

Sir Ensor's House. (Now Lorna's)

A figure is huddled in the throne chair wrapped in a blanket

There is a knock on the door. The figure struggles up. We see that it is Gwenny. She staggers to the door

Gwenny Who be there?
John (*off*) 'Tis I, Gwenny. John Ridd.
Gwenny Liar. How could it be? The valley be cut off by the snow.
John I made some special shoes. Now let me in!
Gwenny It do sound like your common voice!
John Open the door and let me see your mistress.
Gwenny (*opening the door ajar*) Show me first these special shoes.

John holds out a snow shoe

Whoy, they be like canoes!
John Now let me in before I catch my death. By cold or by the Doones.

Gwenny unbars the door and lets him in, then quickly puts the bar up again

What's the meaning of this? Is Lorna safe?
Gwenny The meaning is plain enough. Us be shut in here and starving to death.
John You have no food?
Gwenny Don't 'ee say the word "food". They won't give us ought to eat till Mistress Lorna agrees to wed that beast Carver. Ooh, I am so hungry I could eat thee, young man.
John Here, take this crust. (*He hands her part of a crusty brown loaf which he takes from his pocket*)
Gwenny (*snatching it*) Oh thank 'ee, thank 'ee. (*She tears at it hungrily*)
John Where is your mistress?
Gwenny Lying a'bed. She can scarce walk, so weak is she from cold and hunger.
John I must go to her.
Lorna (*off*) Gwenny?
Gwenny Oh Mistress Lorna, look who is here!

Lorna comes in. She has a large shawl round her. She looks very pale and walks with difficulty

Lorna John! Oh John!
John (*taking her in his arms*) Lorna! My poor love. Come and sit down. (*He sits her in the throne chair*)
Lorna Oh John, are you really here? I never expected to see you again. I had made up my mind to die.
John Don't say such a thing. If *you* should die, my life would be ended too.
Lorna Oh, I do love you so.
John (*trying to lighten things*) Not as much as Gwenny here. She even wanted to eat me!
Gwenny (*eating the bread hungrily*) And shall do afore I have done. Your red cheeks put me in mind of a sirloin.
John (*taking out a pack from an inner pocket*) See here, my love, I have brought you something you have never tasted the like of. Smell it first. I have kept it since Twelfth Night.
Lorna (*with delighted incredulity*) A mince pie!
Gwenny A mince pie?
John My sister Annie made it with spice and fruit. Taste a morsel.
Lorna Oh, thank you, God, and thank you, John. Here, Gwenny, you must have some too. (*She breaks off a piece for Gwenny*)

They both eat hungrily with gasps of pleasure

Gwenny 'Tis like holy manna.
John You shall soon have more than mince pie. You shall have the best meal that Annie can cook. And in the warmth of our farmhouse.

Lorna looks at him

You cannot stay here now. Will you come back with me?
Lorna Oh yes, yes, I will.
John And Gwenny, will you come with your mistress?
Gwenny D'you think I'd stay behind?
Lorna But how will we escape?
Gwenny Ay, *we* have no boat shoes.
John I will fetch my new light pony-sledge and bring it back for you.
Gwenny You have picked the right time, for all the Doones be holding a Festival to honour Brute Carver as their new leader.
John So that's why there was no-one guarding the house.
Lorna They thought it needless with the drifts so high. (*She smiles*) They did not know that my brave John Ridd would find a way. How clever of you to think of making snow-shoes.
John (*modestly*) It was nothing.
Gwenny (*from the window*) Oy, look! They are firing Dunkery Beacon!

Act II, Scene 3   49

John (*joining her*) What? They have brought Dunkery Beacon down here?
Lorna Yes. They brought it down before the snow began. Even before poor grandfather's funeral.
John Dunkery Beacon gone? That will cause more outrage in the neighbourhood than a hundred sheep stolen.
Gwenny Look now, the fire is kindled.

The effect of fire flickering is seen in the distance

It will soon light up the whole valley.
Lorna (*as it occurs to her*) And they will surely see us go!
John No, by the time I return, the fire will have gone down and they will be too full of liquor to notice ought else.
Gwenny (*her mouth watering*) Liquor and roast mutton.
John Now listen, both of you. I shall be back in two hours' time. Pack a few things while I am gone, but not too much. And mind you keep that bar across the door, Gwenny. You should be safe while they are feasting, but take no risk. When I return, I will knock once loudly—so— (*he demonstrates*) and then twice very softly. Have you got that, Gwenny? Once loudly, twice very softly. Shall I repeat it?
Gwenny Oh, go teach your grandmother to suck eggs.
Lorna Gwenny! (*To John*) She means nothing.
John (*folding Lorna in his arms*) Goodbye, my love. I will not be long.
Lorna (*concernedly*) John, you do realize the risk you are taking? And your family too? Once Carver discovers I am gone he will surely seek revenge.
John (*grimly*) I shall meet that when the time comes.

Scene 3

Plovers' Barrows' Farm. Evening

A general flurry of activity as the women prepare for Lorna's imminent arrival. Sarah is mistrustful and anxious. Betty is behaving as if royalty were expected

Lizzie (*at the window*) He is gone nearly two hours now. They should be back.
Annie Pray God they have not been discovered.
Betty Imagine! Sir Ensor Doone's granddaughter coming to a humble place like this.
Sarah She should think herself fortunate.
Betty If John had said the King himself were coming I could not be more shook.

Lizzie (*putting on her cloak*) I will go up to the gate. See if I can spy the sledge.
Sarah (*calling after her*) Now don't catch cold, Lizzie. Not content with stealing my son, she will cause my youngest daughter to catch her death.
Annie Oh Mother, don't talk so.
Betty I had best put the mutton in the oven.
Annie And there are some good sausages left on the blue dish, Betty.
Betty Sausages! Mistress Doone cannot eat sausages.
Sarah I don't see why not. If she means to be a farmer's wife, she must take to farmer's ways.
Annie I am sure she will eat whatever John desires.
Betty But not sausages!
Sarah There are no better sausages than ours.
Betty Lord a'mercy! I still cannot believe it. Such a high-born creature setting her heart on a simple lad like our John.
Sarah A simple lad who has faced great dangers and risked his own life for her.
Betty Ay, I 'spec she has been favouring him from gratitude.
Annie I am sure she loves him as greatly as he loves her. And that is a considerable amount.
Sarah Oh yes, she has him under her thumb, I can see that. Doubtless she will soon be turning me off the farm.
Annie Oh no, Mother!
Sarah And much will *you* care. You will be off with that scoundrel Tom Faggus.
Annie Not without your blessing.
Sarah I see my time is over. Lizzie and I will have to seek our fortunes elsewhere. We are to be abandoned.
Annie Will you have the kindness not to talk such nonsense. Why everything here belongs to you, and so, I hope, do your children.
Sarah Not when they come under the spell of a Doone. Has John forgot that it was one of her kin who killed his father? Well, I have not. And sausages are too good for her.
Lizzie (*running across the yard*) Quick, quick, they are here. The sledge is coming down the lower slope.
Betty (*grabbing the broom*) I had best go sweep back the snow for her.
Annie (*amused*) You've already done that twice, Betty.
Betty (*going out*) There have been a few more specks since then.
Annie Come on, Mother. Let us go and greet her.
Sarah You go if you wish. I shall remain here.

Annie and Lizzie hurry out. Sarah takes off her apron and nervously pats her hair. We hear John's halloo off. Sarah resists the temptation to join the

Act II, Scene 3

others. The girls wave as the sledge approaches. General improvization: "Here they come." "Can you see her?" "There's someone getting out."

After a moment, John appears pulling the sledge. Lorna lies back wrapped in a crimson cloak, the hood covers her face. Gwenny, who has jumped off, follows behind, carrying some bundles. She will hang back as Betty, Lizzie and Annie go to help pull the sledge into the yard

John Quiet now. Easy. The cold and roughness of the track was too much for her.
Annie Poor soul.
Lizzie May we look at her?

They gather round as John pulls back her hood

Betty Lor', but 'er be a beauty!
John Out of the way now while I carry her in. Betty, see to Gwenny there.
Betty (*looking at Gwenny disparagingly*) Who be she?
Gwenny (*with equal animosity*) Who be *you*?
Annie (*to Gwenny*) You must be Lorna's brave little friend who left the signals. Let me take those. (*She goes to take the bundles*)
Betty (*to Annie*) You're not carryin' nothing, Mistress Annie. (*She grudgingly takes the bundles*) 'Ere. And mind you don't bring snow into the house.

John carries Lorna over the threshold. He sees Sarah

John Here she be, Mother. Scarce awake.
Sarah Put her by the fire.
John (*lowering Lorna into a chair*) It's all right, my darling. (*He rubs her hands*)

The others stand round looking at her

Lorna (*regaining consciousness*) Where am I?
John Safely home. This is my mother.

Lorna struggles up

No, my love, stay still.

But Lorna walks across the room to where Sarah is standing. She kneels slowly at her feet

Sarah (*won over*) God bless you, my sweet child. (*She lifts Lorna up*)
John (*as Narrator*) Thus Lorna came to live on the farm. And soon she had won everyone's heart with her gentleness and grace. In spite of the cold outside she felt only the warmth of our love. And a great relief that Carver could not come prowling after her while the snow lay piled between us.

We hear birdsong

At last spring came and the ice started to melt, causing the rivers to rise over meadow and field. The snow crashed down from the rocks bringing all in its wake. And the floods began to roar and foam in every trough and gully. (*Beat*) Then the following day we heard a sound that made our spirits leap.

A horse whinnies off

Annie runs in

And across the moor galloped Tom Faggus. Never minding the state of the roads.

Tom and Annie fall into each others arms

There was great ado between him and Annie. As you may well suppose after four months' parting. And he had such news to tell us that even Mother must be glad.

They move into the kitchen

Scene 4

Plovers' Barrows' Farm. Spring 1684

Tom holds out a parchment as the others, except Betty and Lorna, gather round

Tom There it is. Written in black and white. A royal pardon! (*To Sarah beguilingly*) And if His Majesty can overlook my past misdeeds, then so, I hope, can you, dear cousin.
Sarah (*looking at the parchment*) I cannot understand a single word of it.
Tom Blame the lawyers.
John Ay, they take delight in covering their tracks with dead-leaf words.
Annie Oh Mother, see. There is the King's stamp to prove it.

Act II, Scene 4 53

John It looks genuine.
Tom And so it is. (*He puts an arm round Annie*) Annie shall have a husband who is the pattern of honesty.
Sarah And where will she live, pray? On the highways?
John Ay, Tom, she shall not leave here unless you can provide a home that is fit for her.
Tom The matter is already settled. I have not wasted these four months. Squire Faggus—as now I have right to be called again—has purchased some land to the south of the moors.
Annie (*excitedly*) Old Sir Roger Bassett's farm!
Tom 'Tis a fine piece of pasture, well fit for the breeding of horses.
John And where will you get your horses after this dread winter?
Sarah Ay, it has ruined everyone.
Tom (*airily*) Oh? It did *me* well enough. But then I had Winnie to help me.
Lizzie How mean you?
Tom (*having got his audience*) Well, it was this way. I shod her in a special fashion and taught her to go forth in the snowy evenings and to whinny to the forest ponies who were seeking food and shelter. Never a night did pass when she did not return home with a score or more of ponies.

General reactions of amazement

Then I would lure them into my cattle-pen.
Lizzie How?
Tom By neighing. For I myself can neigh in a manner which will win the heart of the wildest horse. (*He demonstrates*)

We hear Winnie neighing off in answer. They all laugh and exclaim

I have gotten home three hundred of them now.
John Three hundred horses!
Tom Worth ten pound a piece from the dealers.
Lizzie But how did you get the fodder for such a herd in that weather?
Tom Little Lizzie! Sharp as ever. (*Extravagantly*) Why I fed them upon straw and sawdust.
Lizzie Star dust more like.

They all laugh

Tom So do we have your blessing, Cousin Sarah? (*He lays on the charm*) Or may I call you Mother? Oh, it will be fine for me to have a mother again. Had I had someone like you those past years, I might never have strayed from the straight path.

Sarah (*relenting*) Well ... since you have put your evil ways behind you, I suppose I can make no objection.

General embracing and hand-shaking

Annie (*excitedly*) I must go and tell Lorna.
John (*going*) I will fetch her down.

John goes out

Tom I am curious to see John's Lorna Doone.
Sarah She is no Doone, that I do swear. There is not an ounce of evil in her.
Annie No, she is the sweetest, gentlest creature.
Lizzie And she knows more books than anyone I have met.
Tom That is surely a recommendation! A maid who...

John leads Lorna in. She wears a simple dress with the glass necklace round her throat and John's ring on her engagement finger

Tom will notice the necklace at once

John Lorna, I would like to present my father's cousin, Tom Faggus. Er— Squire Faggus as he now is.
Tom Mistress Doone. (*He takes her hand and holds on to it as though mesmerised*) This is indeed a pleasure.
Lorna (*embarrassed*) I have heard much about you, Squire Faggus.
Tom Well, it is all in the past now. I am a reformed character.
Sarah I should not let him sup with you, were he not.
Annie (*to Lorna*) He has been pardoned by the King and has bought some land and we are to be wed soon.
Sarah Not *too* soon.
Lorna (*embracing her*) Oh Annie, I am so glad.
John (*not liking the way Tom is staring at Lorna*) Now Tom, while the womenfolk prepare our supper, shall we take a walk?

They go out into the yard while the women start to prepare the meal

Lorna What may *I* do?
Sarah You are not to do anything, my dear. It is not expected of you. Come sit by the fire.

Lorna goes reluctantly

John and Tom pause in the yard

Act II, Scene 5

Tom Your Lorna Doone is a very beautiful maid.
John You did not have to stare at her so.
Tom It was not for that I stared. Tell me, what know you of her history, John?
John Little more than you. She was brought up as Sir Ensor's granddaughter, but her birth is a mystery.
Tom You realize that by keeping her here you put your family at risk, for the Doones will surely burn you in your beds.
John Doone Valley is flooded now. They cannot leave it.
Tom But it will not be flooded forever. Is she really worth it, John? Her beauty will not always last.
John (*angrily*) Her beauty is the least part of her goodness, and I will thank you for your opinion when I ask it, Tom Faggus.
Tom Bravo, our John. I reckon I'd say the same if I were in your shoes. Nevertheless, in the name of God, do not let the hapless maid go about with a thing worth half the county on her.
John What? Oh, you mean that ring I bought her in London. Why it only cost— —
Tom Tush the ring! I would never have stopped anyone for that. I am speaking of her necklace, you great oaf.
John That glass thing she had as a child?
Tom Glass indeed. They are the finest diamonds I ever set eyes on. And I have handled a good many.
John Diamonds!
Tom That necklace is worth all your farm put together. Ay, and all the town of Dulverton. Trust me, good cousin, for knowing brilliants when I see them. Find out from whence they came, and you will find out who is Lorna Doone.

Scene 5

Exmoor

The sound of birdsong. Lambs bleating. Water running

John and Lorna enter, well-wrapped against the cold, hand in hand

John See. This is the very spot I came looking for loaches that day.
Lorna (*with a fearful note*) And up there Bagworthy Forest.
John Ay. If I had not ventured up there and found the waterfall I should never have met you. Oh Lorna, that was a good day for us.

They embrace

Lorna If only...
John If only what?
Lorna Now that the snows are melted, they will surely seek revenge.
John Doone Valley will be flooded still. They will not be able to attack us.
Lorna But once the waters are subsided...
John John Ridd is more than a match for Carver Doone. Has he not Lorna's love to sustain him?
Lorna He has that. But will it be enough, John?
John With Jeremy Stickles' help it will.
Lorna The King's messenger?
John He has sent word that he is soon to return to this district to find out the temper of the people, whether they be for King or Pope or otherwise. He and his troopers will set up headquarters at our farm. So you need not fear, my love.

They kiss

Lorna You must go now, John. You have work to do.
John Enough to save me from idleness. We must have lost four months' labour.
Lorna I wish you would let me help. In the house, if not the farm.
John I have told you, my love, you are not to do anything.
Lorna But I want to. Why should I be treated differently from your sisters?
John Because you *are* different. Your birth makes you so.
Lorna My birth? Would that I knew the truth about my birth and who I really am.
John The truth is written in your face and in your whole being. I did not need a diamond necklace to tell me you are far above us.
Lorna (*tentatively*) John... I had that dream again last night.
John The coach in the mist?
Lorna And the waves crashing down. Only it was more clear this time. I was in the coach myself. As a small child. Someone was holding me in their arms. A woman. With dark hair.
John Your mother?
Lorna I think not. For when I woke up I was calling for another. "Nita! Nita!"
John Nita? A strange name.
Lorna Strange, and yet... Oh, if only I could remember. (*She turns back to him*) Go now, John, or you will lose *more* labour.
John Come. I will take you back to the farm first.
Lorna Not yet. Let me stay here for a while and watch the baby lambs.
John Well, not for long. I do not want you to get another cough. Promise me now.
Lorna (*teasing him*) Yes, my lord. I will obey your every command.

Act II, Scene 5

John (*laughing as he goes*) You had best do so.

Lorna watches him go, waving

(*Off; calling to his dog*) Watch! Watch! Here, boy.

The dog barks. Lorna turns to look at the lambs. The bleating reaches a peak

Lorna (*laughing*) Oh, you pretty things! (*She starts to pick some primroses. As she does so she sings to herself*)

Suddenly a shadow falls across her path. It is Carver

She looks up and sees him

(*With a gasp of horror*) Carver!
Carver (*with a cruel smile*) Why Lorna, you do not seem very pleased to see me.

She makes to run, but Carver raises his gun

Wait!

She stops

And where might you be going? I have not finished with you yet. (*He points the gun at her heart*)
Lorna No, please, no!
Carver Now let me see. Shall I kill you straight off with a bullet through the heart, or shall I let you die slowly as you deserve?

Lorna is unable to speak. She lets out a little whimpering sound as she waits for him to shoot her. Carver slowly lowers the gun, inch by inch, till it points to the ground

(*Laughing at her terror*) I shall spare you this time, but take heed. Unless you are back at Doone Gate by this time tomorrow, and pure as when that fool, John Ridd, took you away, your death is here. (*He taps the breech of his gun*) Goodbye for now ... my queen.

Carver turns and strides away

Lorna breaks down sobbing, then runs off

Scene 6

Plovers' Barrows' Farm. Next day

John comes into the yard with Jeremy Stickles who is dressed in the uniform of an army captain

Jeremy So if I understand you rightly, John, the situation is this. You think that when Lorna does not return as bidden, the Doones will attack the farm.
John Ay. And waste no time about it. For they must know your troopers are not yet arrived.
Jeremy 'Tis likely then that they will come tonight.
John I fear so.
Jeremy If their valley is still flooded as you say, it is unlikely they will muster more than a few men. Probably the same devils who chased me on my way here.
John At least they cannot burn the farm down. The thatch is still too wet.
Jeremy How many men have you?
John Five, aside from Jem Fry and ourselves. Three of our farm workers, the parish clerk and the cobbler. The constable has lent his staff but will not come himself because there is no warrant.
Jeremy Let me see them.
John (*calling*) Jem!
Jem (*off*) Yes, Master?
John Bring the men to Captain Stickles.
Jem (*off*) Yes, sir. Line up for inspection if you please.

Jem enters, followed by the five men. He carries an old blunderbuss. The three labourers carry a sickle, a flail and a pitchfork. The cobbler carries the constable's staff and the parish clerk brandishes his pitch-pipe. They line up and salute

A pause as Jeremy looks at them

Jeremy A motley crew to be sure.
John They are good men and resolute, united all in hatred of the Doones.
Jeremy Our only hope will be to take them by surprise. We will need to keep watch all night.
John Someone had better sit in yon tree that overlooks the valley. They will likely cross the stream there.

Gwenny appears at the kitchen door

Gwenny I will do that, Master.

Act II, Scene 6

They all turn

John No, Gwenny, this be men's work.
Gwenny Tosh! You know I can climb a tree as well as any man. And *they'll* be needed for the fighting.
John Very well. But make sure the other women stay safe in their rooms.

Betty appears at the door

Betty If *she* be allowed to help, then so be I.
John Now Betty——
Betty Being superior to her in age and length of service.
John You will keep watch in the kitchen then, in case any Doone tries to enter the house.
Jeremy If you have quite done with your domestic arrangements, may we discuss our plan of campaign?

The Lights dim as they all go off

Pause. The hooting of an owl. Bring up moonlight

After a moment, Gwenny comes rushing to where John is stationed

Gwenny (sotto voce) Master, Master. There be a party of 'em just crossed the water below. They be creeping up by the hedgerow now.
John Tell the others to stand by.

Gwenny dashes off

A pause

Carver and six other Doones enter quietly from the back of the auditorium

Carver (*pausing to listen and look around*) The place is quiet. The fools asleep. And it will be the last sleep for some of them too. Are you all here?

General assent

Now listen. Two of you go and make us a light to cut their throats by. I want every man killed. There are two daughters. You may take them off if you please. Only remember one thing. If anyone touches Lorna I will stab him where he stands. Go then. And let Plovers' Farm soon be Plovers' grave.

The Doones approach the farm

At a signal from Jeremy they are set upon by Jem and his men

The battle might be played for comedy and to the accompaniment of suitable music. Appropriate lines can be added later if needed. During the course of the battle, two Doones are killed and two captured. One will try to enter the house and be hit over the head by Betty. Another is about to cut Jem's throat when Gwenny leaps on him from a height. And we should see John save Jeremy Stickles' life in a suitably spectacular way. Carver and the remaining two Doones are about to make off when John steps into Carver's path. John goes up to him and pulls his beard

John Do you call yourself a man?

Carver goes for his pistol but John is too quick, kicking it from his hand

Now listen, Carver Doone, you murdering villain. You have shown yourself a fool by your contempt of me. I may not be your match in cunning, but I am in strength.

Carver It is you, John Ridd, who has grossly misused *us* by your creeping treachery and by carrying off our queen.

John I took her because you starved her and imprisoned her. Take warning now. Come not near her again, for next time I will not show such mercy. Now lie low in your native muck. (*He throws Carver on the ground with a wrestling trick*)

Seeing him down, the other two run off. One turns back and shoots at John

He clasps his arm and we see he is bleeding. Carver gets up

Carver (*as he goes*) May you rot in hell, John Ridd, and I shall be the one to put you there.

Carver disappears into the dark

Jeremy and the others approach. They are leading two prisoners

Jeremy Are you all right, John?
John Yes. 'Tis only a flesh wound.
Jem Make haste, let us pursue them.
Jeremy No. The advantage would be upon their side with only the moonlight. We have done well enough. Two Doones dead. Two prisoners who will be sentenced at the next assizes. And a rude blow to their supremacy. The rest can wait till we have reinforcements.

Act II, Scene 6

They go out

John (*as Narrator*) Soon after the Battle of Plovers' Barrows' Farm, another important matter called our attention. Annie's marriage to Tom Faggus. For Mother agreed to the match at last, in spite of misgivings as to Tom's steadiness. They were married in the church at Oare and went to live in the parish of Molland. (*Beat*) Lorna and I longed to wed too, but she was yet too young. And then there was the question of her rightful parentage. (*Beat*) We were surprised the Doones did not attack us again, for Captain Stickles and his troopers had gone southwards, leaving only three men to protect us. (*Beat*) Then on the eighth day of February we heard grave news. King Charles the Second was dead.

Sound of death knell

And had been succeeded by his brother James, who many feared would bring us back to Papacy. Almost before we had put off our mourning clothes there came rumours of plots and a rebellion in these parts. Led by the Duke of Monmouth.
Annie (*off*) John! John!

He turns and sees her hurrying into the yard carrying a baby in her arms

John Annie! What are you doing here? *And* with the baby?
Annie Oh John, I am in such trouble.
John What is it? Do not cry.
Annie Tom has gone off with the Duke of Monmouth's rebels.
John To fight against the King?
Annie They say the Duke has landed in Lyme Regis and proclaimed himself the rightful heir.
John Oh my God.
Annie I begged him not to go, but he rode off at daybreak. Oh John, you must go after him.
John Be not in such haste.
Annie There is no time to be lost. He will be killed, I know he will. What chance will they have against trained soldiers?
John The fools! The fools!
Annie Oh, say you will go and seek him. For *my* sake and for your godson's. Please.

During the following, Lorna comes and leads Annie off

John (*as Narrator*) I might have refused Annie's plea for the sake of Lorna's safety, had I not heard that the Doones had thrown in their lot with the Duke of Monmouth and most of them had joined the rebels.

John moves away

Even so I was uneasy as I left the farm.

John reappears on horseback

It seemed at first a wild goose chase, for I did not know where Monmouth's rustic army was... I made inquiries, but most of the time I was given false information. I was sent in succession to Bath, Frome, Wells, Wincanton, Shepton, Bradford, Axbridge, Somerton—and at last Bridgewater.

Sound of guns and trumpets off

Where, guided by the sound of guns and trumpets, I rode out of the narrow ways and into the open marshes.

Fog rolls in. John flounders in a bog during the following

Soon a fog came down, so that, although I could hear the sound of conflict, I could not get to it. At last, almost despairing of escaping from this nightmare of spongy banks, I arrived at a hamlet. There I found a guide who led me by many intricate ways to the rear of the rebel army.

The morning sun comes up

We came upon a broad open moor where the summer sun, arising wanly, showed us the ghastly scene.

Scene 7

Battlefield. June 1685

As the sun rises and the mist disappears, we see the battlefield. The battle is over. Bodies are strewn about. Some dead, some dying. Still clasping their pathetic weapons. A pickaxe, a billhook, a scythe

One man passes John, carrying the body of a wounded friend

Man Wend 'ee home, young man. No use fighting any more. All's up with Monmouth.

Act II, Scene 7

John Have you come across a man called Tom Faggus?
Man Faggus the highwayman? No. Methinks he will have lost his magic now, as have we all.

The man goes

John searches amongst the bodies, looking for Tom and calling his name. He sees one that looks like Tom, but it is not him. John lays the man down again, crossing himself. A pause. Then he hears a neighing off

John (*recognising it*) Winnie?

Another neigh

Winnie! (*He goes to her*) Oh Winnie mare, 'tis glad I am to see you. Where is your master? Take me to him. (*He follows Winnie to where Tom lies, badly injured. He kneels down*) Tom? Tom?

Tom groans

Thank the Lord you are alive— It is I, John.
Tom (*weakly*) John!
John Annie sent me to fetch you back, you madman. My God, what a gash! Here, let me staunch the bleeding. (*He pulls a scarf from his neck and ties it tight around the wound in Tom's side*)
Tom (*trying to say something*) Is—is…?
John Don't try to talk. Here. Drink some brandy.
Tom (*drinking*) You have watered it down!
John That's our Tom. Even at death's door you can tell neat liquor.
Tom Is that my Winnie?
John Ay. It was she who brought me to you.
Tom Is she hurt?
John Sound as a roach.
Tom Then so am I. Put me upon her back, John. She will take me home.
John No, you will surely bleed to death, even if you stay in the saddle.
Tom Set me on her back I say. I am safe with Winnie under me. (*He struggles to get up*)
John But Tom, there are soldiers everywhere.
Tom Who will be able to come near me with my Winnie mare? A mile of her gallop is worth ten years of my life.
John (*helping him on to the horse*) Up you get then. Easy now. Place your feet in the stirrups. That's it. Now let me tie them under her body so you cannot be thrown. (*He ties Tom's feet together with a kerchief*) Now lean

forward, Tom. It will stop your wound from bleeding. Right, Winnie, take him home.

Tom   God bless you, John. And look out for yourself.

Tom and Winnie go

John   (*as Narrator*) They galloped off, and I wished I too had a magic horse, for my own was badly foundered. I left her, and set my mind to getting away unharmed.

Soldiers are heard approaching

John dives into a ditch

The soldiers pass by singing drunkenly

Intermittent shooting off and a groan as someone falls. John continues on, then stops as he sees a man hanging from the branch of a tree

Kirke   (*off*) Halt! Or I shoot.

John turns and sees Colonel Kirke approaching with his sword drawn. He is a grim-faced man of about forty. He is followed by some of his men

What have we here? Another rebel, and a big one too! We should get double reward for him. Speak sirrah, who are you? And what will your mother pay for you?
John   I am no rebel, sir. I am on the King's side. An honest farmer.
Kirke   Ha ha. A farmer, are you? Those fellows always pay the best.
John   I will pay naught, for I have done no wrong.
Kirke   Then come, good farmer, to yon barren tree, and you shall make it fruitful. (*He indicates the tree with man hanging from it*)
John   No sir, I beg Your Worship. I speak the truth. I am a loyal servant of the King, harmless and innocent of any acts of— —
Kirke   As loyal as that poor innocent, I warrant. And he is harmless now. (*To the soldiers*) Tie him up.

The soldiers go to tie John. He lashes out, knocking one of them to the ground unconscious

Very well. If you would rather have it so. (*To the soldiers*) Shoot him where he stands and cast his body in the ditch.

John struggles, but is restrained. The soldiers line up and raise their guns

Act II, Scene 7

On the count of five you will meet your maker. One. Two. Three. Four. F— —

Jeremy appears from afar

Jeremy Hold your fire, Colonel! In the King's name. (*He approaches*) Wait, I beg you. Do not kill that man.

The soldiers pause, lowering their guns

Kirke (*angrily*) How now Captain Stickles. Dare you come between me and my lawful prisoner?
Jeremy Nay, hearken one moment, Colonel. For your own sake hearken.
Kirke (*to the soldiers*) Do not shoot him till I give the order. You had best have good reason for this intervention, Captain.
Jeremy Pray give me your ear, Colonel Kirke. The matter is of utmost secrecy.

They go into a huddle

John (*as Narrator*) Phew! Then he went aside with Jeremy Stickles. I could not catch what passed between them, but fancied I heard the name of Lord Chief Justice Jeffreys spoken more than once.
Kirke (*turning back*) Then I shall leave him in your hands, Captain Stickles. But mark you, I shall hold you responsible for his custody.
Jeremy Yes, sir. (*He salutes*) John Ridd, you are now in my custody.

The soldiers untie John

Follow me.

John turns to salute Colonel Kirke but he has now spied some other rebels

Kirke (*to the soldiers*) Make haste, I see some other scoundrels yonder. (*Going off*) Halt there, or I shoot.

John turns to Jeremy and shakes his hand

John Oh, thank you, my good friend. You saved my life.
Jeremy Turn for turn. You saved my life from the Doones. But tell me, what are you doing here? You are no rebel.
John I will tell you as we go.
Jeremy Let us find somewhere to eat and rest first, for I am near famished.

John (*as Narrator*) I was eager to find fresh horses and to ride straight home to my sweet Lorna, but Jeremy's stomach was persistent and since he had just saved my life I did not like to quarrel. So we repaired to an inn on a little foreland near Watchett town. And to this day I know not what great stroke of chance led us to *that* resting-place...

Benita, a handsome Italian woman of about forty, brings on a table and chairs aided by a young maid

The sound of the sea is heard in the background. Gulls

Scene 8

An Inn

Benita leads John and Jeremy in

Benita (*with a pronounced Italian accent*) Please be seated, gentlemen. My husband will attend to the needs of your horses, and I to yours.
Jeremy Then I warrant we have the best of the bargain!

Benita laughs

John (*sitting wearily*) Ah, this is welcome rest. (*He will be preoccupied with his own thoughts during the following*)
Jeremy Indeed. Now what of food, good madam?
Benita I fear there is little, sir, except of common order. We have bacon.
Jeremy Bacon! What could be better?
Benita And fresh laid eggs.
Jeremy Give us a dozen at least.
Benita Cooked my special way with a little garlic.
John Garlic? No, thank you. I prefer my cooking plain.
Jeremy (*to Benita*) His tastes are more rustic than mine.
Benita But *you* will have garlic, sir? With your eggs and bacon?
Jeremy You make me rage with hunger, madam. Is it cruelty or hospitality?
Benita (*laughing*) I will tell my little maid to fetch the frying pan and eggs, while I bring you some ale.
Jeremy Take not too long or I will *ail* for you.

Benita goes out laughing

I have always got on with foreign women better than your Molls and Pegs.

Act II, Scene 8   67

They appreciate my elegance of manner. I wonder by what strange hap a handsome woman such as she should have settled in this lonely inn with a boorish countryman for husband.

John does not react

John? Must I talk to the air?
John Forgive me. My mind was with Lorna.
Jeremy Love! There is nothing like it for coddling the brain.

Benita returns with ale, which she will pour during the following

Benita Here is your ale, gentlemen. It is fresh drawn.
John Thank you.
Jeremy Excellent. Tell me, madam, from what country are you come to these parts?
Benita From Italia.
Jeremy I knew it. The warmth of the south is written all over you. But how come you to England? Let alone a place like this?
Benita It is a long story and one which I fear would spoil your supper.
Jeremy Then pray leave it till later.
Benita Where are *you* from, sir?
Jeremy London. I am a commissioner for the King.
Benita (*dramatically*) Oh God be praised! You are the one I have been waiting for all these years.
Jeremy That is very flattering, madam, but I fear your husband would— —
Benita I knew the good Lord would answer my prayers and send me a man of skill and honesty. Say you will bring my case to justice!
John (*his interest now roused*) What case?
Jeremy Madam, I know not— —
Benita The magistrate here he will do nothing. He says that I am a wicked woman with the cracked brain.
Jeremy (*uneasily*) Indeed?
Benita And I know for why. It is because I am not English. But I say to him, "You think I would of my own will, live in this horrible country where half the year is snow and ice and half is rain and fog?"
Jeremy Pray, madam, calm yourself.
John And tell us your story if you will.
Jeremy But let it be quick, for my stomach is impatient.
Benita I know not where to begin. When I am grown I go to Rome to seek employment in a big hotel. After a year there came to the hotel a rich and noble English family eager to see the Pope. They also were escaping from some quarrel in England. I know not what it was.

Jeremy Then pray progress to what is pertinent.
Benita This noble family they offer me to look after their children. A little boy and his sister.

John reacts

Oh, I did love them so with their pretty ways and the style of their dresses.
Jeremy Spare us the dresses!
John You say you were employed by this noble family. Who were they?
Benita The Earl and Countess of Dugal. I travel with them to the South of France. And then one day—as we approached the Pyrenees, my lord, he galloped ahead of the carriage to see the view and— (*her voice cracks*) we never saw the poor gentleman again. Not alive. He was thrown from his horse, over a precipice.
Jeremy Good madam, do not distress yourself.
John What happened after that?
Benita My lady was persuaded by her friends to return to England.
Jeremy And *you* went with her?
Benita How could I leave her? And those poor children? Oh, they were so beautiful. Especially the little girl. (*She stifles a sob*) Forgive me, but there is worse to come.
Jeremy Then make it brief.
John Go on!
Benita We landed on the coast of Devonshire and set out in a hired coach for Watchett where my Lady owned a small mansion. The weather it was worse even than usual. The coach it drove through fog and mud until we came to the seabank leading on towards Watchett town. The little boy he sleep in his mother's arms, the little girl in mine. And then—oh, I cannot bear to think of it.
John (*with urgency*) You *must* if we are to help you.
Benita Then—through the mist—we saw a troop of horsemen under a rock, waiting to dash upon us. Fierce men they were, and near as tall as you. (*She indicates John*)
John The Doones!
Jeremy (*now equally intent*) It must have been. Continue, madam.
Benita The coachman he tried to drive the horses on, but these robbers they seized them and killed him and the other servants. Then they started to open our boxes and to take my lady's jewels. I quickly snatched the most valuable piece. It was a——
John A necklace of diamonds.
Benita (*looking at him*) How did you know?
John Never mind.
Benita I threw it over the little girl's neck, covering it with her travelling

cloak. And then a great wave crashed down and turned the coach on its side and all was blackness. The last thing I heard was the little girl calling my name "Nita, Nita!" She could not say *B*enita. When I recovered my senses, the robbers had gone, with all our things. I saw my mistress lying dead, her little dead son in her arms.

John (*urgently*) And the little girl?

Jeremy Please, madam, it is important.

Benita I do not know. Either she too was killed and taken by the sea. Or the robbers carried her off. Oh, my poor little Lorna.

John The truth at last!

Jeremy (*beat*) Tell me, madam, would you recognize the child, were you to see her now as a grown maid?

John (*as Narrator*) So Lorna was reunited with her old nurse. And Jeremy Stickles left for London forthwith, carrying messages to the Court of Chancery that she might claim her rightful heritage.

Scene 9

Plovers' Barrows' Farm

John (*as Narrator*) Meantime, the Doones began to plunder the countryside again. In one week alone, they took twenty sheep, a fat ox, two stout deer, three score bushels of flour, two hogs' heads, a half of cider, a hundred weight of candles. And not content with that, two of the maidens in the neighbourhood. (*Gravely*) And then we heard news of a thing much worse, which turned all our hearts sick. The case of Mistress Margery Badcock.

Margery Badcock sits on a stool feeding her baby

A hearty and upright young woman. With one of the finest hen roosts anywhere. She was nursing her child about six o'clock and looking out for her husband, when suddenly six armed men burst into the room.

Six Doones, led by Carver, burst in

Finding naught but a loaf and an onion or two, they took to other sport.

The following to urgent musical accompaniment. Carver grabs the baby from Margery. As she runs to retrieve it, he throws it to another Doone. It is thrown from man to man as the poor woman dashes about desperately reaching for it. Then it falls to the ground as someone drops it. Dead silence. Margery kneels, then holds the baby to her with a terrible moan

Carver Quick. Let us go. (*To Margery*) If anyone asks who killed your baby, say it was the Doones of Bagworthy.

The Doones rush out

The rest of the company—farmers and Ridds—converge from all sides with cries of revenge

First Farmer The Doones must be punished.
Crowd Kill them, kill them.
Margery As they killed my baby.
Sarah My husband.
Annie ⎱ (*together*) Our father.
Lizzie ⎰
Lorna My mother and brother.
Second Farmer They must be destroyed.
Third Farmer Ay, stamped out.
First Farmer Once and for all.
Jem We must get recruits from Barnstaple.
Second Farmer And Tiverton.
Third Farmer And Dulverton.
Jem For there is not a man in these parts who has not suffered at their hands.
Margery Destroy them, destroy them.
First Farmer Who will be our leader?
Jem John Ridd.
Second Farmer Yes. John, you must command us.
Third Farmer Say, will you lead us against the Doones?

General urgings

John Very well, my friends. If it be your wish.

They cheer and raise him up on to a cart

(*Silencing them*) But I make one condition. That we take good care to burn no innocent women or children. They must all be brought out unharmed.

General agreement

And Counsellor Doone must be spared too.

General protest

Not because he is less of a villain than the others, but because he is less violent.

Grudging agreement

We will wait till Friday night for our assault, because then the moon will be out full. This is my plan. In the next days we will cause it to be spread about that a large heap of gold is now collected at the mine at Wizard's Slough. This should delude from home a number of the Doones. On the night of our attack, most of you will fall to—or so it will seem—at the entrance to Doone Valley. While you keep them busy there, a small party, led by me, will enter the Valley from the rear by means of the waterfall. By the time we have set fire to their houses, they will think we are a hundred at least.

As the crowd disperse, the Lights will start to create the burning of Doone Valley

Scene 10

Doone Valley

As John and the chosen few set fire to the houses, we see the women and children running to safety. And we hear the crackling of the fire together with the sounds of fighting in the distance at Doone Gate

John (*chivvying women and children*) Hasten now. Take the children down to the river.
Woman (*running past him*) Help—help—all Doone Town is on fire!
John (*stopping her*) Go quickly to the gate and tell your menfolk that there are a hundred more soldiers behind us.
Woman (*running*) Quick—quick—there are a hundred soldiers burning our houses, with a dreadful great giant at the head of them!

The woman exits

One of John's men goes to set fire to Carver's house. John stops him

John No, wait. This is Carver Doone's house. Leave that to me. But first I must make sure there are no women inside. They say he has taken many so-called wives since Lorna left. (*He calls*) Halloa! Is anyone in there?

No reply

Come out quick, before you are burnt to death.

Another pause, than a very small boy comes out. He is Ensie Doone, fair and handsome

(*Gently*) Why, who are you? Do not be afraid. What is your name?
Ensie Ensie.
John Ensie! I have heard of you. (*To his comrade*) Lorna has spoken most fondly of him. They say Carver is his father.
Man (*heatedly, raising the gun*) Then let Carver Doone know what it is like to lose a chil— —
John (*stopping him*) No! You heard my orders. A child cannot answer for the acts of his father. Come, Ensie. Climb up on my back and I will see you safe. (*He helps Ensie on to his shoulders*)

As they go off, the man makes to set fire to Carver's house. There is the sound of fighting off

(*As Narrator*) That was a night of fire and slaughter and very long harboured revenge. Enough that ere the daylight broke the only Doones left alive were Counsellor and one other. (*Beat*) Carver alone escaped...

The auditorium reverberates with the pounding of hooves

Lo, he dashed through the whole of us at full gallop, and spurring his great horse passed into the darkness.

Bring up daylight

Little Ensie had lost his mother at birth, so he stayed with Lorna here on the farm, and took as much liking to me as his father had of hatred.

Ensie runs on, carrying John's wedding coat

During the following, John will take off his working jacket and put the coat on

In the fullness of time, the case of Lady Lorna Dugal came up before the Lord Chief Justice Jeffreys, who seeing his way to a heap of money made her his ward. And so amused was he that this wealthy and beautiful maid would have no rich young lord, preferring plain John Ridd, that he gave permission, then and there, for us to wed.

Act II, Scene 11

Ensie runs out shouting "Hurrah!"

Bring in wedding music

Scene 11

Oare Church. Spring 1686

Church wedding music plays

The parson stands in front of the altar. John waits nearby with Tom Faggus (his best man) at his side. The congregation includes Sarah, Betty, Gwenny, Benita and her husband, Jem, other labourers, farmers and local gentry

As the music swells, Lorna enters on the arm of Jeremy Stickles. Annie and Lizzie are matron-of-honour and bridesmaid respectively. Lorna should look like the dream bride. John and Lorna meet at the altar. NB: The following is taken from the Anglican wedding service used in 1685. More or less can be used, as desired

Parson John, wilt thou have this woman to thy wedded wife, to live together after God's ordinance in the holy estate of Matrimony? Wilt thou love her, comfort her, honour, and keep her, in sickness and in health; and forsaking all other, keep thee only unto her, so long as you both shall live?
John I will.
Parson Lorna, wilt thou have this man to thy wedded husband, to live together—after God's ordinance in the holy estate of Matrimony? Wilt thou obey him, and serve him, love, honour and keep him, in sickness and in health; and, forsaking all other, keep thee only unto him, so long as you both shall live?
Lorna I will.
Parson Who giveth this woman to be married to this man?
Jeremy I do.

The parson receives Lorna and puts John's right hand over Lorna's

Parson Now John, repeat after me the following words. I John, take thee Lorna, to my wedded wife.
John I John, take thee Lorna, to my wedded wife.
Parson To have and to hold from this day forward.
John To have and to hold from this day forward.
Parson For better, for worse; for richer, for poorer.

John For better, for worse; for richer, for poorer.
Parson In sickness and in health.
John In sickness and in health.
Parson To love, and to cherish, till death us do part.
John To love, and to cherish, till death us do part.
Parson According to God's holy ordinance.
John According to God's holy ordinance.
Parson And thereto I plight thee my troth.
John And thereto I plight thee my troth.

The parson puts Lorna's right hand over John's

Parson And now, Lorna, repeat after me. I Lorna, take thee John, to my wedded husband.
Lorna I Lorna, take thee John, to my wedded husband.
Parson To have and to hold from this day forward.
Lorna To have and to hold from this day forward.
Parson For better, for worse; for richer, for poorer.
Lorna For better, for worse; for richer, for poorer.
Parson In sickness and in health.
Lorna In sickness and in health.
Parson To love, cherish and obey, till death us do part.
Lorna To love, cherish and obey till death us do—— (*She breaks off with a gasp as a shot rings out from the back of the church*)

John catches her in his arms as she slumps. General reactions of horror. Blood seeps through her bridal gown. Sarah goes to John's side

John Lorna! Oh my love, my love.
Lorna (*faintly*) John—I—I... (*She sinks back into his arms as if dead*)
Sarah Oh my God ... she is dead.
John No, no! Lorna—my love—my wife... (*He holds her to him*)
Parson (*shaken*) Who would do such a thing?
John (*with deep emotion*) There is but one man in the world. (*He turns to Sarah*) Take her, Mother. Annie. And lay her on our marriage bed.

They take her

    While I go forth to find the devil who has killed her. (*He holds his arms up and shouts*) Carver Doone!

The words echo all around as the Lights go out

Scene 12

Exmoor. A bog

NB: This is only a rough indication of the scene. Additional dialogue can be added when the method of staging has been decided

The chase. As John follows Carver across the moor. The name "Carver Doone" echoing everywhere. Suddenly we see, with John, the giant shadow of Carver on horseback against the sky

John Come, Carver Doone. You shall not escape me. For there is no room on the entire earth for both of us.
Carver (*shouting back*) True. But try to shoot me and you will shoot the boy.
Ensie (*off*) John! John!

We see Carver holding up Ensie

John (*gasping*) Ensie! Would you hide behind a child?

A shot rings out. John falls to the ground

After a moment, Carver approaches

Carver (*to Ensie*) Stay with the horse, boy. While I finish off Master Ridd. (*He comes near with his gun trained*)

John suddenly springs up, grabbing the branch of a tree. He knocks Carver to the ground. For a minute he is winded

John (*quickly*) Come here, Ensie. No! Stay away from the bog. Go round the edge. Good boy.

Ensie joins him

Ensie Don't let Carver take me away. I want to go home with you.
John (*grimly*) We cannot go home yet. I have business to complete. Run up yonder, round the corner. There's a good lad.

Ensie hesitates

Go on. See if you can find some bluebells.

Ensie goes

Carver struggles to his feet

Now Carver Doone, your life or mine. As the will of God may be!

They fight till they are both close to collapse. They find themselves in the bog and starting to sink. John clambers out and collapses on the ground. Carver lets out a terrible cry as the bog sucks him down. John holds out a hand to him but Carver cannot reach it. He disappears into the bog

A pause. Silence

Then Ensie runs in

Ensie (*seeing no sign of Carver*) Has he gone away?
John Yes, Ensie. He has gone.
Ensie Look, I have picked some bluebells for Lorna. May we take them to her now? (*He looks at John*) Why are you crying?

Scene 13

Plovers' Barrows' Farm

John limps into the yard with Ensie at his side. He is muddy, exhausted, bloodstained

Annie, hearing them approach, comes out, followed by Gwenny

Annie John! We have been so anxious.
John (*to Ensie*) Go, Ensie. Gwenny will attend to you.

Ensie runs to Gwenny who leads him away

Annie Thank God you are alive.
John Alive, but might as well be dead.
Annie No!
John Without Lorna I have no life. (*He turns away burying his head in his hands*)
Annie But John—dear brother, listen to me—she is not dead.
John (*slowly*) Not dead?

Act II, Scene 13   77

Annie No. She is very weak from the loss of blood, but the doctor says she may live. Sure *now* she will.

John rushes into the house. Lorna lies on a bed, Sarah attending to her

John Lorna!
Lorna (*weakly*) John—my husband.
John Thank God, thank God. (*As Narrator*) Thus ends our story. And it ends happily ever after as all the best stories do. (*Beat*) As the years went by our love increased and brought us children of our own. Who oft would sit in the firelight while I told them the tale you have just heard. Of how I first met, and came to love, their mother—known in those far off days as "Lorna Doone".

CURTAIN

FURNITURE AND PROPERTY LIST

Further dressing may be added at the director's discretion

ACT I

Scene 1

On stage: Skeleton of a tree

Off stage: Goods from market, staffs (**All**)

Personal: **Charlie:** gun (carried throughout)
All: purses, hats (some optional)

Scene 2

On stage: Table
Chairs
Large oven
Fire in grate
Long sides of bacon hanging up to smoke
Kitchen utensils
Crockery
Cutlery

Off stage: Black cloak (**Lizzie**)
Throne chair and other props (**Doones**)

Personal: **John:** pipe

Scene 3

On stage: Pebbles on path
Plank bridge across stream
Dice game
Throne chair
Piece of tapestry and leather books (optional)
Chest with drawer. *In it:* small leather bag containing coins

Lorna Doone

Off stage:	Billhook (**Ensor**)
Personal:	**Ensor:** hedger's gloves **John:** blindfold **Sarah:** blindfold

Scene 4

On stage:	As Scene 2 Book **John**'s fishing gear
Off stage:	Gun (**John**)

Scene 5

On stage:	As Scene 1 Rod with three-pronged fork attached at its end Rock **John**'s shoes and socks Basket Bag Fish (rubber model)

Scene 6

On stage:	Flowers
Off stage:	Bottle of liquor (**Charlie**)
Personal:	**Lorna:** handkerchief

Scene 7

On stage:	As Scene 2 Book

Scene 8

On stage:	Bush Mossy tree trunk Stone Fern and moss decoration

	Sweep of ivy 2 large stones
Off stage:	Bunch of early primroses (**Lorna**)
Personal:	**John:** eggs **Lorna:** handkerchief **Carver:** gun (carried throughout)

Scene 9

On stage:	As Scene 2 **Labourers'** packs of tools etc. **John's** jacket for London
Off stage:	Document (**Clerk**) Parchment (**Jeremy**)

Scene 10

On stage:	Papers File

Scene 11

On stage:	As Scene 8 Summer flowers and leaves
Personal:	**John:** ring

Scene 12

On stage:	As Scene 3 Curtain drawn over barred window Rough lattice covering window bars
Off stage:	Lamp (**Carver**)

Scene 13

On stage:	Tree with seven rooks' nests

Lorna Doone

SCENE 14

On stage: As SCENE 3
Box containing glass necklace

Personal: **Doones:** guns
Ensor: loose red cloak

ACT II

On stage: Snow

Off stage: Shovels, sheep (**Labourers**)

SCENE 1

On stage: As ACT I, SCENE 2
Snow
Sheepskin
Snow shoes (set out of sight)

Off stage: Book (**Lizzie**)

SCENE 2

On stage: As ACT I, SCENE 3
Bar across door

Personal: **Gwenny:** blanket
John: crusty brown loaf
Lorna: large shawl
John: mince pie

SCENE 3

On stage: As ACT I, SCENE 2
Lizzie's cloak
Broom

Off stage: Sledge (**John**)
Bundles (**Gwenny**)

Personal:	**Sarah:** apron
	Lorna: crimson cloak with hood

SCENE 4

On stage:	As before
Off stage:	Parchment (**Tom**)
Personal:	**Lorna:** glass necklace, engagement ring

SCENE 5

On stage:	As ACT I, SCENE 1
	Primroses

SCENE 6

On stage:	As ACT I, SCENE 2
Off stage:	Old blunderbuss (**Jem**)
	Sickle (**Labourer 1**)
	Flail (**Labourer 2**)
	Pitchfork (**Labourer 3**)
	Constable's staff (**Cobbler**)
	Pitch-pipe (**Parish Clerk**)
	Baby (**Annie**)
Personal:	**Doone:** knife
	Betty: stick
	John: fake blood
	Doone: gun

SCENE 7

On stage:	Bodies
	Weapons: pickaxe, billhook, scythe, etc.
	Manikin hanging from tree
Off stage:	Table and chairs (**Benita** and **Young Maid**)
	Wounded friend (**Man**)

Personal:	**John:** scarf
	John: kerchief
	Kirke: sword
	Soldiers: guns

Scene 8

Off stage:	Ale, glasses (**Benita**)

Scene 9

On stage:	As ACT I, Scene 2
	Cart
Off stage:	Baby (**Margery**)

Scene 10

Off stage:	Lit torches (**John** and **Others**)
	John's wedding coat (**Ensie**)
Personal:	**Man:** gun

Scene 11

On stage:	Altar
Personal:	**Lorna:** fake blood

Scene 12

On stage:	As ACT I, Scene 1
	Bog

Scene 13

On stage:	As ACT I, Scene 2
	Bed

LIGHTING PLOT

Property fittings required: lamp
Various interior and exterior settings

ACT I, Scene 1

To open: Moonlit night lighting

Cue 1   **Second Farmer**: "Oh my God."   (Page 2)
          Shadows of horsemen outlined against the sky

Cue 2   **Ridd** turns towards the ridge   (Page 4)
          Bring up effect of moon spotlight on horseman outlined against the sky

ACT I, Scene 2

To open: Overall general lighting, fire effect in grate

*No cue*s

ACT I, Scene 3

To open: Overall general lighting

*No cue*s

ACT I, Scene 4

To open: Overall general lighting

*No cue*s

ACT I, Scene 5

To open: Cold spring day lighting

Cue 3 **John**: "...and the cold grew worse and worse." (Page 16)
         Fade lights

Cue 4 **John**: "For lo, between two cliffs, was a huge waterfall." (Page 16)
         Create waterfall with lighting

ACT I, Scene 6

To open: Overall general lighting

No cues

ACT I, Scene 7

To open: Summer lighting

No cues

ACT I, Scene 8

To open: Early spring lighting

Cue 5 **Carver** smashes the eggs (Page 25)
         *Black-out, then bring up lights on **Lorna**'s bower*

ACT I, Scene 9

To open: Early evening lighting

Cue 6 **John**: "...ten days later, in excellent condition." (Page 30)
         Dim lights

Cue 7 **John**: "...preferring to see London by daylight." (Page 30)
         Bring up lights

Cue 8	**John**: "…might assail her in my absence." *Spotlight on* **Gwenny** *at white rock, high up*	(Page 31)

ACT I, SCENE 10

To open: Summer lighting

*No cue*s

ACT I, SCENE 11

To open: Overall general lighting

Cue 9	**Gwenny** positions herself to keep watch *Bring up lights on* **Lorna**'*s bower*	(Page 36)
Cue 10	**John** moves off *Dim lights*	(Page 38)

ACT I, SCENE 12

To open: Hazy moonlight, faint gleam from upper window

Cue 11	**Lorna**: "…lest you should think me false." *Fade moonlight down then up*	(Page 39)

ACT I, SCENE 13

To open: Winter lighting

*No cue*s

ACT I, SCENE 14

To open: Overall general lighting

*No cue*s

ENTR'ACTE

To open: Lights up on John

Cue 12   **John**: "And then came the snow…"   (Page 44)
           Snow effect

ACT II, SCENE 1

To open: Early morning lighting

No cues

ACT II, SCENE 2

To open: Overall general lighting

Cue 13   **Gwenny**: "Look now, the fire is kindled."   (Page 49)
           Bring up effect of fire flickering in the distance

ACT II, SCENE 3

To open: Evening lighting

No cues

ACT II, SCENE 4

To open: Spring lighting

No cues

ACT II, SCENE 5

To open: Overall general lighting

No cues

ACT II, Scene 6

To open:	Overall general lighting	
Cue 14	They all go off *Dim lights*	(Page 59)
Cue 15	An owl hoots *Bring up moonlight*	(Page 59)
Cue 16	**John**: "…to the rear of the rebel army." *Bring up morning sun*	(Page 62)

ACT II, Scene 7

To open: Rising sun lighting

*No cue*s

ACT II, Scene 8

To open: Overall general lighting

*No cue*s

ACT II, Scene 9

To open: Overall general lighting

Cue 17	The crowd begins to disperse *Gradually fade up effect of Doone Valley burning*	(Page 71)

ACT II, Scene 10

To open: Burning houses effect

Cue 18	**John**: "…passed into the darkness." *Bring up daylight*	(Page 72)

ACT II, SCENE 11

To open: Spring lighting

Cue 19   **John**: "Carver Doone!"   (Page 74)
           Fade out lights

ACT II, SCENE 12

To open: Overall general lighting

Cue 20   **John** follows **Carver** across the moor   (Page 75)
           *Bring up effect of giant shadow of **Carver** on horseback against the sky*

ACT II, SCENE 13

To open: Overall general lighting

*No cue*s

EFFECTS PLOT

ACT I

Cue 1	To open SCENE 1 *Mist; sound of tumbling stream nearby, bleating of sheep in the distance*	(Page 1)
Cue 2	**Ridd** turns towards home *Gunshot*	(Page 4)
Cue 3	To open SCENE 2 *Sound of sheep bleating off, dog barking, hens clucking*	(Page 4)
Cue 4	**Betty** and **Annie** are preparing dinner *Gunshots in the distance*	(Page 13)
Cue 5	To open SCENE 5 *Sound of water, sheep bleating, birdsong*	(Page 15)
Cue 6	**Annie** goes out *Sound of sheepdog barking off*	(Page 16)
Cue 7	**John**: "…and saw in front of me a great black pool." *Sound of waterfall*	(Page 16)
Cue 8	**John**: "…which came from the far end." *Peak roaring water sound*	(Page 16)
Cue 9	**John** ascends the waterfall *Dramatic music (optional), crash of waterfall*	(Page 16)
Cue 10	To open SCENE 6 *Sound of a stream, birdsong*	(Page 17)
Cue 11	To open SCENE 8 *Sound of birdsong, rippling of the stream*	(Page 23)
Cue 12	**Carver**: "There's no-one here." *Fade up single birdsong above the rest*	(Page 25)

Cue 13	**Carver** shoots at the bird *Cut birdsong*	(Page 25)
Cue 14	**Labourers** leave *After a pause, sound of horse neighing off*	(Page 27)
Cue 15	**John**: "...preferring to see London by daylight." *London noises*	(Page 30)
Cue 16	**John**: "...left in secret places by Gwenny Carfax." *Bring in mist*	(Page 37)
Cue 17	To open SCENE 12 *Mist; sound of owl hooting off*	(Page 38)

ACT II

Cue 18	**John**: "And then came the snow..." *Snow effect*	(Page 44)
Cue 19	**Labourers** enter carrying sheep *Plaintive bleating of sheep*	(Page 44)
Cue 20	**John**: "...while the snow lay piled between us." *Birdsong*	(Page 52)
Cue 21	**John**: "...a sound that made our spirits leap." *Horse whinnies off*	(Page 52)
Cue 22	**Tom** neighs *Horse neighing off*	(Page 53)
Cue 23	To open SCENE 5 *Sound of birdsong, lambs bleating, water running*	(Page 55)
Cue 24	**John**: "Here, boy." *Dog barking*	(Page 57)
Cue 25	**Lorna** turns to look at the lambs *Peak bleating*	(Page 57)
Cue 26	They all leave *After a pause, hooting of owl*	(Page 59)

Cue 27	**Jem** and his men attack *Suitable music (optional)*	(Page 60)
Cue 28	**John**: "King Charles the Second was dead." *Sound of death knell*	(Page 61)
Cue 29	**John**: "…and at last Bridgewater." *Sound of guns and trumpets off*	(Page 62)
Cue 30	**John**: "…into the open marshes." *Bring in mist*	(Page 62)
Cue 31	The sun rises *Disperse mist*	(Page 62)
Cue 32	**John** crosses himself *After a pause, horse neighing off*	(Page 63)
Cue 33	**John**: "Winnie?" *Another neigh*	(Page 63)
Cue 34	**Soldiers** pass by singing drunkenly *Intermittent shooting off*	(Page 64)
Cue 35	**Benita** and young maid bring on table and chairs *Sound of sea in the background, gulls*	(Page 66)
Cue 36	**John**: "…they took to other sport." *Urgent music*	(Page 69)
Cue 37	Women and children run to safety *Crackling of fire, sounds of fighting in the distance*	(Page 71)
Cue 38	**Man** makes to set fire to **Carver**'s house *Fade up sound of fighting off*	(Page 72)
Cue 39	**John**: "Carver alone escaped." *Loud pounding of hooves*	(Page 72)
Cue 40	**Ensie** runs out *Wedding music*	(Page 73)
Cue 41	To open SCENE 11 *Church wedding music, increasing in volume*	(Page 73)

Cue 42	**Lorna**: "To love, cherish and obey till death us do——" *Gunshot from back of church*	(Page 74)
Cue 43	**John** follows **Carver** across the moor *Echoes of "Carver Doone"*	(Page 75)
Cue 44	**John**: "Would you hide behind a child?" *Gunshot*	(Page 75)

www.ingramcontent.com/pod-product-compliance
Lightning Source LLC
LaVergne TN
LVHW051750080426
835511LV00018B/3290